Department of Economic and Social Affairs

Unlocking the Human Potential for Public Sector Performance

World Public Sector Report 2005

United Nations
New York, 2005

DESA

The Department of Economic and Social Affairs of the United Nations Secretariat is a vital interface between global policies in the economic, social and environmental spheres and national action. The Department works in three main interlinked areas: (i) it generates, compiles and analyses a wide range of economic, social and environmental data and information on which Member States of the United Nations draw to review common problems and to take stock of policy options; (ii) it facilitates the negotiations of Member States in many intergovernmental bodies on joint courses of action to address ongoing or emerging global challenges; and (iii) it advises interested Governments on the ways and means of translating policy frameworks developed in United Nations conferences and summits into programmes at the country level and, through technical assistance, helps build national capacities.

Note

Symbols of United Nations documents are composed of capital letters combined with figures.

ST/ESA/PAD/SER.E/63
ISBN 92-1-123155-8

Foreword

There has been a rediscovery in recent years of the critical role played by human resources in improving and sustaining institutional effectiveness and development performance. It is this realization that has provided the impetus to focus the *World Public Sector Report* on this important topic. Governments increasingly look at public administration reform as a key instrument to achieve important development goals and to catalyse wider transformation in society. At the same time, public administration will not be able to play this role effectively without competent and dedicated public servants. This means that the management of human resources has moved to the fore as a central concern of leaders in the public service.

This *World Public Sector Report* surveys some of the major trends, models and related visions that have influenced human resource management practices around the world in recent decades. It highlights the diversity of values and doctrines that have guided the strengthening of HRM systems in the public sector. The present report advocates that future reform in this area involves striking a balance between three broad models or schools in public administration: *traditional public administration; public management,* including *new public management* (NPM); and an emerging model of *responsive governance.* An important objective of the report is to discuss how the best attributes of these three models can be effectively harnessed to address contemporary challenges facing HRM in the public sector worldwide.

The theme *"Unlocking the Human Potential for Public Sector Performance"* is particularly pertinent at this point in time when the interconnectedness of professional management of human resources and government effectiveness has become very evident to leaders and managers in the public service in both developed and developing countries. The report hopes to further stimulate debate, particularly in developing countries and transition economies, on how to manage human resources in the public sector more effectively for enhanced development performance and social progress.

The report is also intended to serve as a substantive input into a number of upcoming intergovernmental meetings where the role of public administration in facilitating the realization of the Millennium Development Goals will be on the agenda. It is similarly expected that the report will contribute to discussions at a Special Session of the General Assembly in 2006, which will review progress in revitalizing public administration during the past ten years, or since the adoption of the landmark General Assembly resolution 50/225 on public administration and development.

JOSÉ ANTONIO OCAMPO
Under-Secretary-General for Economic and Social Affairs
October 2005

Preface

At the core of the process of realizing the Millennium Development Goals (MDGs) is a new vision for development that places people at the centre of socio-economic progress in all countries. This vision also recognizes the important role of global partnership and solidarity in enabling developing countries to achieve the MDGs. While some countries are on track in achieving the goals, many more are still lagging far behind.

The report demonstrates that the development performance of countries is heavily underpinned by the quality of public institutions. Effective public institutions make it possible for governments to coordinate human action for the public interest. When public institutions perform well, it is primarily owing to the motivation, skills and integrity of the human capital and the quality of leadership. In other words, people are the lifeblood of the public service and the main source of its vitality and strength.

Thus, the strengthening of national capacity for public administration is one of the best measures that governments in developing countries can undertake in their efforts to realize the MDGs before the year 2015. More specifically, the report argues that capacity development of public servants needs to move to the centre stage in institution-building in developing countries and transition economies. It also makes excellent economic sense for governments to invest in greater professional development of staff, particularly career civil servants, who are generally lifelong employees of the state. This realization has unfortunately often been lost in the negative debate in both developing and developed countries on the role of the public sector in society—a debate that has tended to portray public servants primarily as a cost that can be slashed rather than as an asset that will grow in value if properly nurtured and utilized.

The report also highlights that institutional transformation in the public sector involves the individual transformations of public servants. Changing the values and attitudes of public servants is never easy and will require principled leadership and a clear vision and strategy for human resource development. It will also call for more professional management of staff in the public service. One important objective of publishing the *World Public Sector Report* is to join the call for greater professionalism in public administration in developing countries, with special emphasis on the management of human resources.

One of the constraints impeding strategic management of public servants and highlighted in the report is the lack of systematic collection and analysis of data on the quantity, quality and performance of human resources in the public sector. This issue will increasingly have to be addressed by governments at both the national and the global level. Without continuous, accurate, reliable and valid data on human resources in the public sector, critical human resource management decisions will already be obsolete when implemented. Instead, the planning for the public sector of tomorrow should be based on the present and projected state of human resources.

GUIDO BERTUCCI
Director of the Division for Public Administration and Development Management
October 2005

Acknowledgements

The third *World Public Sector Report* (WPSR) was finalized under the guidance and direction of Guido Bertucci, Director of the Division for Public Administration and Development Management of UN/DESA. Within the division, Kristinn Sv. Helgason was the editor-in-chief and principal coordinator of the report. He was supported by Vilhelm Klareskov, who contributed to most aspects of the report, as well as a team composed of Ke Lu, Sarah Waheed Sher, and Mila Gorokhovich. Administrative support was provided by Gracia de Leon-Dizengoff.

A number of background papers shaped the preparation of the WPSR. Many ideas and country examples originated in such papers prepared by Martin Painter, Willy McCourt, Gerald Caiden, Randhir Auluck-Cooper and Farhad Analoui. Martin Painter as the lead resource person also provided guidance on the report, which is hereby gratefully acknowledged. Larry Willmore, former senior staff member of UN/DESA, prepared the background paper for the technical summary and provided advice throughout the process.

The WPSR team received expert inputs, such as drafting of text boxes, technical advice, and encouragement, from a task force of in-house colleagues chaired by John-Mary Kauzya and composed of Nahleen Ahmed, Adriana Alberti, Elia Armstrong, Jide Balogun, Alphonse Mekolo, Olivier Munyaneza and Gay Rosenblum-Kumar. Technical advice was also provided by G. Shabbir Cheema and Jerzy Szeremeta, both of UN/DESA. A group of external reviewers provided comments and suggestions on an early draft of the report. The group consisted of Jocelyn Mason, Public Administration Adviser, UNDP; Dimitri Argyriades, former senior official of UN/DESA; John Lawrence, former senior official of UNDP; Neil Reichenberg, Executive Director of the International Public Management Association for Human Resources; and Joao Paulo Peixoto, former Chief Technical Adviser of the REFORPA Project of UN/DESA in Angola. We are also grateful to Marc Levy of Columbia University for providing data from the State Capacity Survey.

The preparation of the WPSR benefited greatly from discussions and reports of meetings of the United Nations Committee of Experts on Public Administration. The findings and recommendations of the High-Level Capacity Development Workshop "Building the Human Capital in the Public Sector" held at the Fifth Global Forum on Re-inventing Government (Mexico, November 2003) also influenced the key messages of this report. In addition, a series of ad-hoc expert meetings organized by UN/DESA in recent years contributed to the substantive development of the WPSR, in particular, the following: "Unlocking the Human Potential," Florence, May 2004; "New Challenges for Senior Leadership Enhancement for Improved Public Management in a Globalizing World," Turin, September 2002; and "Managing Diversity in the Civil Service," New York, May 2001.

External editing was provided by Barbara Brewka. Fine Composition typeset the report. Advice on the layout and design was provided by Jim Eschinger and Valerian Monteiro.

Executive summary

The main objective of the **_World Public Sector Report 2005_** is to discuss the critical role of people and human resource management (HRM) in effective public administration, with a particular focus on developing countries and transition economies. It is people, coordinated by institutions, who deliver public services. How effectively government institutions align the behaviour of staff with the public interest is determined primarily by the capacity, motivation and integrity of human resources and the quality of leadership. In other words, people are the lifeblood of the public service. This underscores the need to value people highly and to develop and manage human resources with great care.

The field of HRM has evolved significantly in the past decades as external and internal pressures have forced governments to redefine the role of the state and recalibrate public administration capacities. This evolution, while responding to contemporary economic, social, political and technological developments and reflecting current trends in public administration doctrine, builds on a longer history of the theory and practice of public sector personnel management.

As part of this process of evolutionary reform, many governments are currently grappling with the search for a new synthesis of traditional and modern principles and techniques of public administration and management. The present report advocates that this search for a new synthesis involves striking a balance between three broad models or schools in public administration, namely, _traditional public administration; public management,_ including _new public management_ (NPM); and an emerging model of _responsive governance_ that emphasizes networks, greater openness and partnerships with civil society and the private sector. Each one of these models offers principles, tools and techniques that are essential in addressing contemporary challenges facing HRM worldwide.

Thus, an important challenge facing public leaders is how to incorporate or reinvigorate desirable traditional civil service values, such as impartiality, integrity and dedication to public service, while at the same time promoting management innovations and efficiency improvements as well as encouraging more open and responsive forms of administration. The HRM synthesis advocated in this report proposes a public service that is _impartial, professional_ and _responsive_ and that draws, where appropriate, on the skills and resources of the private and civil society sectors. In addition, the new synthesis stresses the need for the public service to curb corruption and to exhibit the highest levels of neutral competence, efficiency and performance orientation in every respect.

In order to realize this vision for HRM reform, the report makes a series of recommendations for consideration by governments in developing countries and transition economies. A few of those messages are highlighted next:

1.   Professionalizing HRM: _towards "strategic specialization"_

Staff responsible for human resources should not be confined to playing a restricted, bureaucratic and reactive role, limited by and large to routine decisions about staff entitlement to pay increments and the like. Instead, they should have real input into strategic decisions about staff management as well as decisions on how to achieve the core objectives of government. This calls for the upgrading of the status and influence of human resource managers in organizational structures and decision-making processes in the public sector.

Strategic specialization implies an all-encompassing approach to workforce planning and development. However, the lack of quality data on employment and wages in the public sector, particularly in developing countries and economies in transition, makes it difficult to measure the actual cost and contribution of staff to the overall performance of the public sector. With a number of socio-economic factors depleting the pool of talent in many countries, it becomes even more critical to improve the collection and analysis of data on the workforce in order to plan prudently for the future.

2.   Merit appointment: *the best person for the job*

Strengthening appointment on merit is one of the most powerful, yet simplest, ways in which governments can improve their effectiveness. A merit-oriented and career-based civil service is decisive in explaining cross-country differences in the performance of governments in terms of the quality of services and the absence of corruption. The presence of these factors helps to foster organizational standards, behavioural norms and esprit de corps that promote commitment and integrity among public servants. The complex internal and external challenges facing the public service in many developing countries, many of which are discussed in the report, also provide a sense of urgency for governments to forge political consensus to establish a merit-based career civil service as part of a national development strategy aimed at promoting sustainable growth and equity. Merit-based HRM policies are also essential to improve and maintain the prestige of public sector employment.

3.   Remuneration: *balancing motivation, equity and ability to pay*

Adequate pay is a key component in improving and sustaining the motivation, performance and integrity of public servants. Thus, the development of a pay policy is an integral part of strategic HRM in the public sector. The goal of such a policy should be to pay public servants enough to attract and retain competent people while providing sufficient incentives for staff to maintain a high level of performance over a sustained period. In a political environment, a delicate balancing act must also be performed by juggling key priorities and interests of stakeholders as well as motivation and equity of staff and the ability of governments to pay when developing a remuneration policy. In short, equitable pay is difficult to achieve without a "rightsized" and professional public service.

One favourite approach of NPM-advocates has been performance-related pay. Evidence on performance-related pay, however, is inconclusive and ambiguous. It is certainly not a panacea for improving public sector performance. In part, this is because it is difficult to implement in the way that the model proposes: assessing "performance" according to measures of efficiency alone is rather hard to achieve. A single-minded focus on material incentives also downgrades other reward and incentive measures that may be just as important.

4.   Performance management: *supporting and developing staff*

Governments need to instil greater performance orientation among public servants. This means that performance management, including staff appraisal, must become central to the work of government managers. The managers are responsible for the performance of staff, and it is their job to manage them by setting objectives that relate to the overall goals of the organization, monitoring their performance, and giving them support, feedback and the opportunity to develop. Strengthening performance orientation in the public service also entails giving greater weight to relative efficiency vis-à-vis seniority in decisions on staff promotion in the public service.

5.   Outsourcing: *a double-edged sword*

Improving efficiency is one of the claimed benefits of outsourcing, with new market-like constraints and incentives pushing managers to lower costs. Yet caution is required to avoid attributing the success of outsourcing to the wrong causes. In fact, savings are due to mainly less favourable pay and working conditions for private sector workers compared to their public sector counterparts. The recent use of outsourcing in the security and military sectors through private military firms and contractors has also been fraught with controversies, in some instances, because of lack of clear policies regarding the regulation of such companies.

6.   New Public Management: *solutions chasing problems?*

NPM as a set of principles and practices has been diffused as a "global model", often assisted by the weight of influential international agencies. The first lesson to be drawn from the experience of NPM is that its world view is not shared by all. Many have pointed out its "Anglo Saxon" origins and the extent to which it is a creature of that culture and its history. An analysis presented in this report concludes that NPM, measured as the mobility of high-level personnel between private and public sectors, has a negative impact on the prestige of public sector careers. Furthermore, there is little evidence that NPM strengthens the quality and integrity of the civil service. In fact, many local problems in developing countries are quite different from those that NPM seeks to solve. In some instances, NPM has been described as "solutions chasing problems" when in fact the problems require other solutions.

7.   Leadership in the public sector: *"walking the talk"*

A leadership style based on command and control is no longer suited for effective public sector management. Instead, leaders are increasingly judged by their ability to motivate and bring out the best in staff, by how well they communicate the vision and mission of the organization, and by their effectiveness in building partnerships and collaborating with other organizations. Together, the complexity of challenges in the public sector is requiring new leadership skills of senior civil servants.

Since public sector transformation often involves the reform of values and attitudes of staff, the role of leadership by example is critical. The term "leading by example" indicates the transformational power of leadership when employees follow the example of a leader. An important role of a leader is to champion the shared vision, values, norms and standards of the organization. This will require high-level skills combined with strong commitment and determination on the part of the organizational leadership.

8.   HRM at the crossroads: *challenges and opportunities*

Demographic changes. Populations all over the world are ageing. This poses a critical HRM challenge in the public sector, including the high costs of sustaining public service pension funds. Reducing pension benefits, on the other hand, is likely to decrease the attractiveness of public sector employment and make it more difficult to attract new talent. This is an important consideration since a high proportion of senior civil servants are expected to retire in the next few years in a number of public services, with potentially significant loss of institutional memory and capacity. For this reason, succession planning has emerged as a high priority in HRM in several countries.

Labour migration. The departure of a skilled migrant signifies a loss of investment in previous education and training for the country of origin as well as a loss of skills and experience that would otherwise provide future contributions to development, including future tax payments. In developing countries, it is important that this phenomenon be counterbalanced by "earn, learn and return" strategies to take advantage of the enhanced skills and experience of the expatriate population, with programmes to facilitate remittances and encourage migrants to return. In critical employment sectors, such as health and education, governments also need to adopt specific programmes and incentives to stem the tide.

HIV/AIDS. In some countries, particularly in sub-Saharan Africa, HIV/AIDS is having a staggering impact on the performance of governments. The management of HIV/AIDS issues in the work place presents many dilemmas. Mortality is only one aspect of the problem to be managed. Given that the disease normally affects younger adults and those in the most economically productive phases of their lives, HIV/AIDS has the potential to reduce the pool of prospective employees and economic productivity in many countries. Governments facing such challenges need to adopt a clear employment policy on HIV/AIDS in the work place, addressing issues such as testing, disclosure, absenteeism (including sick pay) and support services.

Contents

Boxes

Figures

Scatter plots

Tables

Explanatory notes

The following symbols have been used throughout the report:

,   **A comma** is used to indicate thousands.

.   **A full stop** is used to indicate decimals.

–   **A hyphen** between years, for example, 1990–2003, includes the beginning and end years.

.. **Two dots** indicate that data are not available.

Reference to dollars ($) indicates United States dollars.

The following abbreviations have been used:

APS	Australian Public Service
BAMF	Federal Office for Migration and Refugees in Germany
BGN	Brain Gain Network
BPE	business per employee
CAFRAD	African Training and Research Centre in Administration for Development
CAP	career assignment programme
CFA	Communauté Financière Africaine (African Financial Community)
CSA	Civil Servants' Association
DPSA	Department of Public Service and Administration in South Africa
DTC	diagnosis and treatment centre
FICCI	Federation of Indian Chambers of Commerce and Industry
GATS	General Agreement on Trade in Services
GDP	gross domestic product
HIV/AIDS	human immunodeficiency virus/acquired immunodeficiency syndrome
HPAE	high-performing Asian economies
HRM	human resource management
IBA	Indian Banks' Association
ICRG	International Country Risk Guide
ICT	information and communication technology
ILO	International Labour Organization
IMF	International Monetary Fund
INR	Indian rupees
INTAN	National Institute of Public Administration in Malaysia
MCSAAR	Ministry of Civil Service Affairs and Administrative Reforms in Mauritius
MINFIB	Ministry of Finance and Budget in Cameroon
MINFOPRA	Ministry of Public Service and Administrative Reform in Cameroon
NGO	non-governmental organization
NHS	National Health Service
NPfIT	National Programme for Information Technology
NPM	new public management
OECD	Organisation for Economic Co-operation and Development
OWWA	Overseas Workers Welfare Administration in the Philippines
PAYG	pay-as-you-go
POEA	Philippine Overseas Employment Administration
PPE	profit-per-employee
PPP	public-private partnership
PRR	performance-related reward
PSC	Public Service Commission

PSMA	Public Service Modernization Act
REFORPA	Institutional Strengthening of Public Administration in Angola
RMC	redeployment management committee
SANSA	South African Network of Skills Abroad
SCS	State Capacity Survey
SES	Senior Executive Service
SIGIPES	Système Informatique de Gestion Intégrée des Personnels de l'Etat et de la Solde (Integrated Computerized State Personnel and Payroll Management System)
TMNP	temporary movement of natural persons
TOKTEN	Transfer of Knowledge through Expatriate Nationals
TQM	Total Quality Management
UN/DESA	Department of Economic and Social Affairs of the United Nations Secretariat
UNDP	United Nations Development Programme
UNU	United Nations University
VCT	voluntary counselling and testing
VRS	voluntary retirement scheme
ZESCO	Zambia Electricity Supply Corporation

The designations employed and the presentation of the material in this publication do not imply the expression of any opinion whatsoever on the part of the United Nations Secretariat concerning the legal status of any country, territory, city or area or of its authorities, or concerning the delimitation of its frontiers or boundaries.

The term "country" as used in the text of this report also refers, as appropriate, to territories or areas.

For analytical purposes, the following country groupings and subgroupings have been used:[a]

Anglo-Saxon countries

Australia, Canada, New Zealand, United Kingdom of Great Britain and Northern Ireland and the United States of America.

Countries with economies in transition ("transition economies")

Central and Eastern Europe

Albania, Bulgaria, Czech Republic, Estonia, Hungary, Latvia, Lithuania, Poland, Romania, Slovakia and successor States of the Socialist Federal Republic of Yugoslavia: Bosnia and Herzegovina, Croatia, Serbia and Montenegro, Slovenia and the former Yugoslav Republic of Macedonia.

Commonwealth of Independent States (CIS)

Armenia, Azerbaijan, Belarus, Georgia, Kazakhstan, Kyrgyzstan, Republic of Moldova, Russian Federation, Tajikistan, Turkmenistan, Ukraine and Uzbekistan.

Developed countries

Europe (excluding the European transition economies)

Canada and the United States of America.

Australia, Japan and New Zealand.

Developing countries

Africa

Asia and the Pacific (excluding Australia, Japan and New Zealand and the member States of CIS in Asia).

Latin America and the Caribbean.

High-performing Asian economies[b]

Hong Kong Special Administrative Region of China, Indonesia, Japan, Malaysia, Republic of Korea, Singapore, Taiwan Province of China and Thailand.

Nordic countries

Denmark, Finland, Iceland, Norway and Sweden.

The designation of country groups in the text and tables is intended solely for statistical or analytical convenience and does not necessarily express a judgement about the stage reached by a particular country or area in the development process.

---

a Names and composition of geographical areas follow those of "Standard country or areas codes for statistical use" (ST/ESA/STAT/SER.M/49/Rev.3).

b This analytical grouping was introduced in the early 1990s. It did not include currently fast-growing economies such as China and Viet Nam.

Towards an Impartial, Professional and Responsive Public Service

Introduction

Within living memory, it used to be fairly simple and straightforward to define the administrative state, to delineate the public sector, to differentiate and distinguish public administration, and to identify the profession of government as consisting of trained and experienced public administrators who devoted their working lives to running public organizations. However, given the speed and scope of ongoing change in most societies, public administration is under a great deal of pressure to adjust and innovate just to keep pace with developments and facts or else it will find itself falling further and further behind the expectations of citizens as well as politicians and other stakeholders.

The changing role of public administration has been influenced by many factors, including the emergence of new tasks and activities for government, the transformation of many of its traditional functions, and the recent revolution in information and communications technology (ICT) that alone is requiring radical change in work, management, and decision-making processes in all organizations but especially in traditional-style bureaucracies. Nonetheless, certain challenges stand out as needing immediate attention lest all other efforts fail to realize their potential. Among these for public administrators everywhere, in both developed and less developed countries, are coping with globalization, restoring the capacity to govern, furthering democratization, adapting to the knowledge society, and attracting talent into public service.

Essential to the capacity of governments to respond to these critical challenges effectively will be renewed focus on the management of human resources, the lifeblood of the public service, including the development of strong leadership capacities. This is the overarching message of the *World Public Sector Report 2005*.

Chapter I

The *first chapter* provides an overview of the evolution and key attributes of three broad models or schools on which most of the lessons and examples of contemporary global thinking about HRM reform are based: *traditional public administration*; *public management*, including *new public management* (NPM); and *responsive governance*. Each of the three models espouses certain core values and key variables that are essential in addressing contemporary HRM challenges.

A new HRM synthesis should build on the best attributes of these three models. Traditional public administration, for example, is anchored in the enduring principles of impartiality and merit; public management places particular importance on performance management and professionalism; and the governance paradigm stresses the need to make public administration more responsive to the demands of citizens and other stakeholders. The present report suggests that the unifying principles of such an HRM synthesis in the public service could be *impartiality*, *professionalism* and *responsiveness*.

Chapter II

The *second chapter* focuses on why the quality of HRM in the public sector is critical for government performance and national development. It emphasizes that reform of HRM will depend on the pre-existing structure of public administration in a given country. Governments are well advised to start HRM reform on the basis of their current needs, developing and adjusting gradually to meet the requirements of the day rather than adopting a blueprint model drawn from an international "best practice". It is this "path-dependent" character of public service institutions and procedures—the result of their history—at least as much as cultural differences that explains why governments vary to such an extent in the basic structures that they have put in place to manage staff. While some countries need to lay the foundations for HRM by putting into place the necessary legal and regulatory framework and ensuring that these policies are being followed, other countries, where the foundations are strong, already have the luxury of building on them, for example by delegating authority to line managers.

Senior officials, unlike their counterparts in the private sector, have traditionally been constrained in the exercise of leadership and taking initiatives by the complex political environment and institutional arrangements in the public sector. Without a solid understanding of the political context, it will be very difficult, if not impossible, for leaders to spearhead comprehensive reform effectively, particularly in environments characterized by significant resource scarcities. In such situations, it is important for leaders to have a good grasp of the complex networks of people that underpin the operation of the public sector.

Chapter III

The *third chapter* examines some of the major socio-economic challenges confronting governments and posing serious questions about the sustainability and integrity of key aspects of public sector human resource systems. A common thread running through these socio-economic challenges is that they affect in some measure both developed and developing countries. The present report examines three prominent challenges with direct consequences for HRM. First, it focuses on demographic shifts and in particular the challenge of an ageing population. Second, the report examines recent trends in labour migration, including the so-called "brain drain". Finally, it looks at the effects of HIV/AIDS on public sector management, especially in sub-Saharan Africa.

Chapter IV

The *fourth chapter* discusses some of the recent HRM reform experiences. Among those discussed in this chapter, the report highlights how structural adjustment and downsizing of the public sector constituted a dominant trend during the 1980s and 1990s in many developing countries. Such measures often resulted in a set of harsh actions that lacked support and legitimacy because of their social impact, to the detriment of other reforms that might have resulted in improvements in administrative capacity. Moreover, only modest results were often achieved beyond the elimination of ghost workers and others who should not have been on the payroll. The lessons learned from NPM are also assessed in this chapter, with a particular focus on the devolution of HRM, outsourcing, performance-related pay and deregulation as well as the relevance of NPM for developing countries. The issues of labour-management relations and diversity management are also briefly discussed in the chapter.

Chapter V

The *fifth chapter* reviews some of the key frameworks, strategies and systems that need to be in place for effective HRM in the public sector. Whether governments need to establish or amend legislation governing civil service employment, the present report advocates that embedding the principle of merit is essential. In addition, it is important that the values of *impartiality, professionalism* and *responsiveness* be institutionalized, promulgated and protected by a prestigious, professional and powerful guardian agency at the centre of government.

Every government needs to develop a policy statement that defines how staff management will contribute to the achievement of its overall strategic objectives. Whatever HRM strategy a government chooses to adopt, it will need to provide professional HRM support to the managers who make staffing decisions. The application of an integrated competence-based model is also an important part of strategic management of human resources in the public service. By promoting a consistent approach across all HRM activities, the framework helps to ensure that HRM contributes effectively to achieving the government's objectives.

Another integral part of strategic HRM is the development of a comprehensive pay policy that enables the public service to attract and retain talent. Adequate pay is widely considered a key component in improving and sustaining the motivation, performance and integrity of public servants. Conversely, low salary levels result in absenteeism, alternative and additional employment, corruption and low productivity. These pros and cons as well as additional challenges of developing a pay policy are discussed in the chapter.

Chapter VI

The *sixth chapter* points out that many observers believe that governments have lacked the ability to learn and adapt to circumstances of rapid change such as those experienced during the last two decades. Governments tend to experience great difficulties in diagnosing problems early, selecting policy directions, designing effective and efficient programmes, rectifying problems and avoiding what is commonly referred to as state or public sector "failure". An important quality of a public sector engaged in organizational learning, on the other hand, is its adeptness in identifying and analysing salient cues in the broader environment as well as in responding to those cues in a strategic, timely and thoughtful manner.

Governments have many ways to promote organizational learning in the public service. On one hand, they can focus on strategies that encourage greater sharing of both explicit and tacit knowledge among staff, and, on the other, they can emphasize incentives for public servants to take more direct charge of their own capacity-building needs within an overall corporate HRM strategy.

The role of leaders in developing an environment of learning and trust is very important. By playing a proactive role in promoting information-sharing and better communication within the organization, leaders can send a message that learning is a high priority and that old ways of doing business are being actively discouraged. Organizational learning can also be facilitated through more effective coaching and mentoring of junior and mid-level colleagues. Several countries, for example, have opted for fast-track programmes where high-flying candidates are put on paths to senior management under the guidance and advice of mentors.

Technical summary

Finally, the *technical summary* provides quantitative analysis that supports the discussion in the main body of the report. By applying linear multiple regressions to cross-country data, the analysis measures the impact of selected variables on the quality and integrity of the public service and on the prestige of public sector employment. It confirms a positive correlation between merit-based recruitment as well as promotion and the quality as well as integrity of the public service, but not the prestige of public sector employment. Better remuneration of senior officials increases the quality and integrity of bureaucracies and enhances the prestige of public sector employment, although the latter is only the case in non-African countries. New public management, measured indirectly by the extent to which senior officials mix private and public sector careers, has no apparent effect on the quality or integrity of the public service. It is associated, however, with low prestige of public sector employment, making it more difficult and expensive for government to recruit and retain a fair share of the best talent. These findings are explained in more detail in the technical summary at the end of the report.

Chapter I
The globalization of public sector reform

The changing role of public administration

The field of human resource management (HRM) has evolved significantly in recent decades as external and internal pressures have forced governments to redefine the role of the state and recalibrate public administration capacities. This evolution, while responding to contemporary economic pressures and reflecting current trends in public management doctrine, builds on a longer history of the thought and practice of public sector personnel management.

In the present report, a distinction is made among three broad models of public administration and management underlying contemporary government HRM reforms: *traditional public administration; public management*, including an important recent development, *new public management;* and *responsive governance*. In some measure, they are chronological, yet they overlap in both historical time and substance. The last of the three—*responsive governance*—is not so much a historical model as an emergent set of trends. Its inclusion reflects a potential convergence of thinking, based on significant developments in practice and new challenges. Table 1 highlights some of the unique characteristics of each one of the three models.

Cutting across these three models are the varied experiences of social and economic development in different eras and in diverse geopolitical environments. For example, in many Western democracies, a rights-based social agenda in the second half of the twentieth century impinged strongly on public sector HRM, particularly through anti-discrimination measures.

> Contemporary HRM reform has been shaped by three main models: public administration; public management and governance

Table 1.
Three models of public administration

	Public administration	**Public management**	**Responsive governance**
Citizen-state relationship	Obedience	Entitlement	Empowerment
Accountability of senior officials	Politicians	Customers	Citizens and stakeholders
Guiding principles	Compliance with rules and regulations	Efficiency and results	Accountability, transparency and participation
Criteria for success	Output	Outcome	Process
Key attribute	Impartiality	Professionalism	Responsiveness

In many contemporary developing countries and transition economies and polities, varying legacies such as colonialism, post-colonialism and state socialism have meant that ideas and principles embodied in the three models, when transplanted, have been modified in quite distinctive ways. Despite these lasting historical legacies, the models provide most of the lessons and examples on which contemporary global thinking about HRM reform is based.

Traditional public administration

Traditional public administration is associated with the emergence of civil service systems in countries undergoing industrialization in the second half of the nineteenth century. These systems embodied a set of rules about merit-based recruitment and promotion, for example, the use of competitive examinations. Other rules covered security of tenure and the payment of a decent, fixed salary, usually determined by job-related criteria rather than by market value. These rules and procedures were often entrenched in the form of laws and regulations that were overseen and implemented by more or less independent personnel authorities.

One of the purposes of this, as with the institutionalization of merit, was to take politics and politicians out of the field of personnel management so as to eliminate political patronage. The important principle was also established that the civil service was an impartial but obedient instrument of the state or of the sovereign (in an increasingly large number of countries, the latter took the form of an elected political executive). Its relation to the public was also that of a detached, impartial interpreter and implementer of the laws and the policies of the day. Thus, the civil service came to enjoy the status of an impartial protector of the public interest and became a symbol of stability and continuity.

There were some important variations within this overall Weberian bureaucratic model of rationalization, functional specialization, and hierarchical organization due to national legal traditions or cultural factors. For example, continental European traditions tended to cloak the civil servant with a distinct legal personality as an embodiment of the state, serving to entrench even more strongly its role as a guardian of the public interest. In the United States, a layer of top officials was politically appointed by the President and expected to be replaced if the party in office was voted out. In Sweden, uniform, permanent civil service forms of employment were confined to a small core service, with other public servants employed under varying terms and conditions by each separate agency. In the United Kingdom, a "class" system was established consisting of the administrative, the professional and the clerical, with different recruitment criteria and promotion prospects for each class. By contrast, in Australia, the base-grade entrant or a technical-cum-professional appointee could rise all the way to the top more easily, with competition for top jobs increasingly opened up to everyone.

Different systems also treated merit differently. For example, there was a strong tendency in some systems to equate fitness for promotion with the length of loyal, disciplined service, in other words, to rely on seniority rather than on the appraisal of relative efficiency. Some systems developed job descriptions and position classifications to regulate appointment, promotion and remuneration, while others relied more on broad-banded systems of rank and seniority.

Despite these national variations, the underlying similarities were more important and defined an increasingly universal model of public service personnel management in the wealthier, and at that time more developed, countries. For the most part, the systems transplanted by the colonizing powers and later inherited by newly independent developing nations followed this model. The modernizing strategies of non-Western countries that escaped colonization, such as Thailand, included the importation of such a civil service sys-

---

Traditional civil service systems were rule and procedure-based

The civil service was seen as an impartial but obedient instrument of the executive

The tendency was to rely on seniority rather than appraisal of relative efficiency in decisions on staff promotion

Most countries adopted traditional civil service systems

tem. In nineteenth century China, the Emperor delegated the customs service to a civil service composed purely of Western officials working independently of the imperial bureaucracy that proved to be much more efficient and less corrupt.[1]

In colonial societies, however, there were important differences. The colonial civil service systems were unequivocally identified with the political interests of the foreign rulers, while the colonial subjects were far from being "equal before the law" and treated impartially by the civil service. These elements were part of the legacy taken over by post-independence ruling elites, when it was necessary to apply various measures to try to redress the situation. Another difference was that the civil service was completely out of step with employment and other conditions in the wider economy and society: it was an enclave of relative privilege and Western modernism.

New political elites were concerned mainly with national mobilization and economic development, for which purposes the civil service was an indispensable tool. In consequence, the civil service in a number of cases became an instrument of political mobilization and patronage, blocking the development of "neutral competence". The public employment system was itself used as a resource to be distributed to followers and the winners of the electoral game, and, as a consequence, civil service systems became heavily politicized. In fact, while civil service systems in post-independence countries structurally resembled those in the former colonial administration, in terms of behaviour, they were different. This phenomenon was sometimes labelled as "prismatic" in the debate on development administration.

Post-independence civil services were enclaves of relative privilege

The civil service in some cases became a spoils system

Public management

From the late nineteenth century, when the United States progressive movement called for administrative reforms such as the separation of politics from administration and the employment of professional managers, the example of business management has had a strong hold on the minds of public sector reformers. This continued to be the case even after patronage and other ills had been suppressed in the development of the modern civil service.

The traditional public administration paradigm of personnel management was quite distinct in important respects from that which prevailed in the private sector. For example, it was much less common for private sector management to offer security of tenure although some large companies did operate a career service system (e.g., in Japan). However, even then, it was more common than in the public sector for relative efficiency to be adopted for promotion and placement purposes and for continuing employment to depend on performance. Perhaps it was easier in business to measure performance although this was not necessarily so, as many of the same kinds of jobs in the public sector—such as legal work—are also found in private firms and have no immediate measurable result with respect to the primary product of the business.

Another difference in the private sector was that pay and remuneration tended to be governed more by labour market conditions; mobility for staff between different employers was also more common. Use of contract or temporary workers was much better suited to the need for flexibility in the market place.

Practices that developed in the private sector were the principal source of the public management model, or "managerialism", as it has sometimes been labelled.[2] This refers to the belief that management is a generic art or science, applicable to any context whether in the private or the public sector. However, business management doctrines and practices are more difficult to categorize as a coherent package than are the components of traditional public administration. They change and adapt as business needs change; they are subject to waves

Traditional public administration was distinct from the private sector

Practices developed in the private sector were the principal source of the public management model

of fashion, which spread across the world often discarding pre-existing local conditions and exhibit constant experimentation.

Public management
has a primary focus
on efficiency
and results . . .

. . . and is driven by
business objectives
and organizational
performance

Yet one enduring theme is the notion that management (not "administration") has a primary focus on efficiency and results. The public management paradigm dislikes rigid rules, formal procedures and uniform systems such as those that prevail in the traditional civil service. It emphasizes the hands-on skills of the manager and the need for managers at all levels to exercise initiative. At the same time, the "science of management" should be brought to bear to help managers to solve generic management problems. Whether adopting doctrines such as Taylorism (treating employees as part of a machine-like production process) or the human relations school (treating employees as people with human needs), the aim is to fit the human resource system into a wider framework of management, driven by business objectives and the requirements of bottom-line organizational performance.

These ideas were espoused by many businessmen and management experts brought in to review government efficiency throughout the twentieth century in both the United States and Europe. The change in terminology from "personnel administration" to "human resource management" as a way of describing and conceptualizing the personnel function in the public sector was a sign of their influence. Under the public management model, diverse sets of HRM practices drawn from management science and doctrine were adopted, depending on the "business needs" or the "business model" of the particular organization. For example, it was claimed that "management by objectives" and "strategic planning" would enable each organization to adapt its HRM practices to its particular objectives and circumstances.

Public management
opposes a one-size-
fits-all approach

The public management paradigm is best characterized not by any particular doctrine or set of practices but by its hostility to the one-size-fits-all approach of the traditional civil service. For some business circumstances, contracting, competition, piece rates and performance pay may be appropriate; for others, the recipe might be more permanent employment conditions, corporate attention to "whole-person development" and a focus on teamwork and work-place solidarity. The paradox, or irony, is that one of the criticisms directed at public management is the way that it sought to impose itself globally, thereby, in fact, promoting a one-size-fits-all approach.

New public management

So-called new public management (NPM) is a modern development within the public management tradition. Its ubiquity and impact on a global scale are undeniable. It not only seems to have dominated academic and practitioner discourse in contemporary public administration, but it has also carried the stamp of approval of influential international institutions disseminating best practices. Much of the value of the NPM currency could be said to have been derived from the ongoing attention to it by organizations such as the Organisation for Economic Co-operation and Development (OECD).

The rapid diffusion of
NPM is an example
of globalization of
public sector reform

As a result, NPM ideas and practices are current in places that are culturally, economically and politically as diverse as Mongolia and New Zealand or Singapore and Zimbabwe. This rapid diffusion of the NPM doctrine is an excellent example of globalization of public sector reform. Exactly because NPM has become a widespread trend in such different settings, caution is advisable in interpreting its significance.[3] One problem is that the label is loosely applied. NPM in this discussion is given a relatively narrow meaning.

First, it is distinguished from "new public policy", that is, those policies adopted by many governments from the 1980s in the name of slowing government growth and reducing the share of the public sector in total gross domestic product (GDP).[4] These policies were adopted by some governments for ideological reasons and by others as their response to the increasing vulnerability of protected national economies in the face of globalization. Governments of the left in Australia and New Zealand from the middle of the 1980s, for example, took up privatization, expenditure cuts, labour-market deregulation and various other forms of structural adjustment in order to survive in challenging economic circumstances.

For developing nations, these so-called "structural adjustment" policies were often externally imposed and reflected an orthodoxy or consensus among international financial institutions and their economic advisers about the steps needed to rescue weakening economies and become viable players in the global economy. However, while there is a distinction, in practice, the "new public policy" paradigm tended to be accompanied by NPM while structural adjustment programmes also incorporated its ideas.

NPM is often associated with "structural adjustment" policies

Second, while NPM is often characterized by its use of business management as a model, this does not set it apart. As already pointed out, business has always been an attractive model for public administration reformers concerned with improving efficiency and service quality. The shift from thinking of public administration as a distinctive enterprise to thinking of it as "public management" both pre-dates NPM and also led to a diverse array of administrative initiatives (including NPM). For example, business models informed the emergence of staff empowerment through participation and teamwork. Total quality management (TQM) is another business improvement model with widespread contemporary influence in many public sectors, for example in Malaysia, where quality had been a major focus of public sector reform, whereas NPM has been less influential.

Business has always been an attractive model for public administration reformers

Some commentators indiscriminately include all such management innovations in their depiction of a very broadly defined "new public management".[5] NPM, however, can also be viewed as both a particular doctrine and a distinctive tool-kit of administrative techniques. As a doctrine, it combines insights from economic theories of institutions with practical lessons from business management, the latter selected because they conform to these theories. While experiences of applying NPM vary from one local setting to the other (as described in chapter III), the "ideal type" of NPM nevertheless subscribes to some basic attributes.

NPM doctrine combines economic theory with practical business management

The theories begin with the assumption that everyone is motivated by the desire to maximize personal preferences. From this assumption, such models as *principal-agent* and the *budget-maximizing bureaucrat* are derived.[6] Thus, in order to align the agent's self-interest with the principal's objectives, both should be monitored according to rules, constraints and performance agreements that incorporate incentives rather than according to the principles of obedience, trust or the building of joint commitments. Once these contractual arrangements are in place, in an agency budget or in a contract of employment, for example, the agent can be left to "self-manage" rather than be instructed or closely supervised.

"Self-management" is preferred to supervision

To take another example, if a government wants to provide just the right amount of a service at the desired quality and at the lowest feasible cost, then market disciplines will provide the right constraints and incentives to bring about this outcome. Hence, such instruments as internal markets, user charges (as distinct from equity or ability to pay) and contestability or contracting out are advocated. Thus, the characteristic tools of NPM are competition, marketization, autonomization, disaggregation and deregulation, all of which embody an anti-bureaucratic philosophy. The fundamental criticism of bureaucracy in this view is that it has no answer to efficiency except more rules and regulations, the usual result of which is greater inefficiency.

NPM embodies an anti-bureaucratic philosophy

Traditional public administration often seems weak when it comes to efficiency

It is important, however, to keep in mind that the world view of NPM is not shared by all. Many have pointed out its Anglo-Saxon origins and the extent to which it is a creature of those cultures. In Europe, some countries have not been attracted to NPM models and solutions. In some cases, this is because they have a "statist" culture and tradition that are not receptive to marketization as a solution to public service problems. Their bureaucra-

NPM is to some extent a creature of Anglo-Saxon culture

cies are imbued with top-down, public law privileges and obligations that cannot so easily be carved up or contracted out. Public bureaucracies and civil servants both enjoy the status and possess the legal and political capacity to resist such suggestions.[7]

Key features of NPM-style HRM

A key feature of NPM-style HRM is the *normalization* of the status of the public sector employee; that is, the legislation and the institutions that made traditional employment in the public administration distinctive are jettisoned or downgraded. In some cases, security of tenure is lost while market conditions are deployed as a primary driver of human resource initiatives. Agency managers are able to strike work-place contracts with their own employees just as a business does.[8] The implications of this include a much smaller role for central regulation of the civil service and, in the extreme case, the abandonment altogether of the concept of a "civil service" encompassing the whole of government.

Another key aspect is the focus on *performance* or output in all aspects of personnel management primarily through such NPM instruments as contracting and "pay for performance". Many of these measures have encountered resistance from established civil service systems and their defenders in case they destroy too much of familiar, traditional forms of public administration. In some countries, such as Australia and New Zealand, implementation of NPM initiatives has been followed by a refocusing on these more traditional concerns.

As discussed in chapter V, there has been a revived emphasis on core capacities and on maintaining continuity and integrity through fostering civil service values, such as commitment to public service. The fear is that something important may be lost when the distinctiveness of the career civil service is blurred through wholesale adoption of private sector practices. The technical summary demonstrates that this fear is not unfounded. In particular, it shows that there is no evidence from the available data that NPM—indirectly measured as the mixing of public and private careers of senior staff—has had a positive effect on either the quality or the integrity of the public sector.

Among the more appealing and universally attractive elements in the array of NPM principles and tools is *customerization*. The growing focus on service quality, or responsiveness to customer or consumer needs and demands, implies efforts to incorporate quality-service and customer-satisfaction indicators into performance measures and appraisal systems and a need to shift some authority and resources to the point of customer interface.

From an HRM point of view, however, a dilemma arises over the conflicting tendencies of top-down agency performance criteria such as efficiency and effectiveness and bottom-up standards of service quality and customer responsiveness. A very familiar conflict between bureaucratic control and professional discretion, especially in areas such as human service delivery, reappears in a new guise. Increasingly, it has been found that many customers of government services are not necessarily best served by NPM-style specialization, disaggregation or contracting out. Such customers (or clients, as they were traditionally known) have many related needs that may be best served by more flexible joint provision of services and service integration. The lessons learned from NPM are discussed in detail in chapter IV.

Responsive governance

While public management originated in an admiration for businesslike efficiency, more recently a new model has evolved that focuses on "creating public value".[9] This view counters the bottom-line mentality derived from many business models and emphasizes a focus on the management of multiple stakeholders and conflicting values in an overtly political or

Margin notes

NPM advocates the "normalization" of status of the employee . . .

. . . and focuses on "performance" of staff

Wholesale adoption of private sector practices has been found to impair the esprit de corps

"Customerization" is a priority on the NPM agenda

NPM is not always the answer

The focus on "creating public value" has emerged as a reaction to the excesses of NPM public-interest context. The significance of such a view of public administration is that it is in part a reaction to what are seen by some as the excesses of NPM, but it also carries the seeds of a wider set of contemporary changes in both thinking and practice.

NPM, perhaps, was based on too narrow a set of assumptions and values. Broader and more inclusive is the set of principles and practices encapsulated by "governance". "Governance" is a catch-all word that entered common usage during the 1990s. The term was first coined in the *1989 World Development Report* where it referred mainly to financial accountability of governments. The meaning of this term was later re-conceptualized by UNDP, defining "governance" as the exercise of political, economic and administrative authority to manage a country's affairs. An important objective of governing institutions, according to UNDP, is to promote constructive interaction between the state, the private sector and civil society. Later, in World Bank and donor discourse, it became a call to arms for advancing a new agenda of development assistance, the perception being that financial or technical assistance would not be put to good use until such concepts as transparency and accountability, due process, probity and efficiency were institutionalized in the systems of government of recipient countries.

"Governance" took centre stage during the 1990s . . .

. . . and became a call to arms for a new development agenda

The governance model raises a set of concerns different from those preoccupying advocates of the NPM model. It emphasizes a government that is open and responsive to civil society, more accountable and better regulated by external watchdogs and the law.[10] A strong role is proposed for "voice" and for civil society "partnerships" through non-governmental organizations (NGOs) and community participation.[11] Governance models thus tend to focus more on incorporating and including citizens in all their stakeholder roles rather than simply satisfying customers, a theme that echoes the notion of "creating public value".

Governance models focus heavily on citizens as stakeholders

New governance theory in the academic discipline of public administration picks up some of the same themes.[12] A strong claim in this body of ideas is that in a more complex, globalizing world, the monolithic Weberian state is being supplanted by, on the one hand, a set of arrangements that rely more on networks than on hierarchy and, on the other hand, by the "post-regulatory state", which relies less on direct provision and heavy doses of government authority and more on lighter, more selective instruments, including a preference for self-regulation and partnerships with non-governmental institutions.

The monolithic Weberian state is being supplanted

Governance theory looks beyond management and service reform by pointing to new kinds of state-society linkages and new, more multilayered and decentred forms of governing (including supranational institutions such as the European Union). Citizen involvement is given a new emphasis through co-production of services (various forms of self-help), a coordinated customer focus in order to address individual needs and problems holistically, and a desire to incorporate the views of citizen groups directly into the service delivery process.

Recent developments emphasize the importance of multiple forms of public accountability

A common theme running through these recent developments is the importance of multiple forms of public accountability. Traditional public administration focused on hierarchical accountability within the civil service and further upward to political leaders. Public management also brought into play professional accountability of the kind that the manager in the public sector acquires through training and experience. NPM focused on the dual, mutually reinforcing accountability to the bottom line and to the customer, while responsive governance depicts diverse, complex forms of 360-degree accountability in which there are multiple stakeholders in both government and society, all of whom have a claim to be heard and answered.[13]

Openness and transparency are thus part of this emerging model. Accountability in the responsive governance model calls for new forms of skills and leadership on the part of civil servants, requiring that they be both politically impartial and socially responsible yet also politically aware and sensitive. Professional and personal ethics may, in such circumstances, be increasingly important and will require increasing attention in future human resource strategies.

Responsive governance calls for politically impartial and socially responsible civil servants

ICTs and responsive
governance are tarred
with the same brush

The responsive governance model is also emerging from a separate but in some ways parallel set of developments in thinking and in practice, namely, the potential impact of information and communication technologies (ICTs) on public administration. ICTs in theory make possible a more dispersed but at the same time a more informed and transparent process of decision-making (box 1). Powerful networks of high-volume communication are at the disposal of individuals and groups, transcending boundaries and barriers—sectoral (public/private), organizational, spatial and jurisdictional. Particular gains are envisaged through the use of ICTs in handling the government-citizen interface via systems that enable two-way electronic communication and secure service-delivery transactions. ICTs might also enable back-office systems integration such that a customer with multiple needs could be handled at one point of contact—a kind of virtual "one-stop shop". All of these potential gains have numerous implications for accountability and responsiveness.[14]

The full utilization of
ICTs requires new
combinations of exper-
tise, accountability and
responsiveness

In sum, the combination of new governance and the information revolution creates a vision of public policy and administration that requires new combinations of expertise, accountability and responsiveness. This vision of *responsive governance* is far from being realized and embodies some utopian elements. In terms of HRM policies and practices, the implications have not yet been clearly articulated. They could include the need for new kinds of expertise and the development of public service cultures that encourage more diverse

---

Box 1

Information and communication technologies

The ICT revolution has the potential to transform government as a whole—with far-reaching implications for human resource management. This transformation is likely to affect the work of governments in four principal areas:

1. Internal processes and relationships both through machine automation of routine tasks—especially record keeping and data retrieval—and through enabling much higher levels of communication and collaboration among members of an organization regardless of physical location (the networked "virtual organization");

2. Relations between government and consumers of services and between employers and employees through electronic service delivery;

3. Relations between government and citizens via various forms of digital democracy, including "virtual communities" that facilitate information exchange and political mobilization; and

4. Relations between government and business through taking advantage of "e-business" opportunities in areas such as procurement.

In human resource management, even the basic applications of ICTs bring major challenges, especially in poor countries. For example, the technical aspects of building online human resource information systems can be solved relatively easily, but effective information systems rest on the integrity and quality of the underlying management systems.

Thus, an integrated online human resource information system will be of no use unless the physical personnel records are already in good order so that they can be transferred to the electronic database. Subsequently, management systems as well as data interfaces must be in place so as to update the records constantly, and the capacity must be in place to input the data correctly at dispersed locations.

For recent resources on the challenges and opportunities facing e-government in developed and developing countries, readers are advised to review the *World Public Sector Report 2003: E-Government at the Crossroads* and the *Global E-Government Readiness Report 2004*.

Sources:
See Bibliography.

forms of knowledge acquisition and dissemination, that is, more sophisticated knowledge management systems and the fostering and development of organizational climates that encourage openness, partnerships and participation as distinct from closure and a primary concern for continuity.

Emerging issues

This survey of models and related visions has highlighted the diversity of values and doctrines that have emerged in the history of wider public sector reform and that, in turn, have influenced public sector HRM practices. How do different countries measure up according to the three models? This is not an easy question to answer with any precision because the three models overlap in places while actual practices and institutions often exhibit a combination of aspects of each. However, it is possible to begin by using as a benchmark those countries that were the first to adopt traditional public administration (they were there "at its birth"), observing, first, the variations in the extent to which they have adopted various forms of public management, NPM and responsive governance.

Among the OECD countries, all have engaged in some degree of public management modernization of their traditional bureaucracies, while they also generally seek to retain the core values of neutral competence that these bureaucracies embodied.[15] It has often been observed, however, that there is a marked variation in the extent to which they have adopted managerialism and NPM doctrine and tools. The Anglo-Saxon countries tended to be more enthusiastic about NPM, while many continental European countries were much more cautious. A middle ground was taken by some of the Nordic countries.

More recently, those countries that adopted NPM most enthusiastically (such as Australia and New Zealand) have rediscovered some of the virtues of traditional public administration and have adapted their reformed, marketized systems accordingly. Many states in East Asia institutionalized most elements of traditional public administration, but they have been somewhat cautious about NPM reforms. Some prime examples of relatively high-performing bureaucracies, such as Malaysia and Singapore, have been enthusiastic borrowers of business management concepts such as TQM but less attracted to marketization NPM-style.

The seeds of the responsive governance model can be found in the United States, with its long traditions of decentralization, self-help and grass-roots democracy. Not surprisingly, the United States is also one of the leaders in the application of ICTs to citizen-government interactions. However, countries that have mastered traditional public administration but that have been less influenced by public management and NPM seem, on the whole, tardier in developing ICT applications. This may be because NPM directly advocates a customer focus and hands-on management as distinct from bureaucratic formalism and detachment. In several surveys of ICT adoption and readiness, the top countries are predominantly Nordic or Anglo-Saxon.[16] However, there are interesting exceptions to the rule, such as the Republic of Korea and some other high-performing East Asian governments, where ICTs are welcomed as a way of modernizing traditional public administration.

Many countries, however, have yet to institutionalize traditional public administration. This is most obviously the case in poor countries, including many in Africa. Often, extreme instability, war or "state failure" has put the process of bureaucratic modernization into reverse, the most striking contemporary example being Somalia. More generally, economic and political strains associated with dependency and under-development have resulted in the decline and decay of many infant civil service systems.

Anglo-Saxon countries were enthusiastic about NPM . . .

. . . while continental Europe was more cautious . . .

. . . with the Nordic countries somewhere in between

The lessons learned from NPM have spurred a rediscovery of basic values

The seeds of responsive governance can be found in the United States

Traditional public administration is yet to be institutionalized in many countries

Another group of countries with a history of turbulent or interrupted administrative development in the twentieth century is the Eastern European transition economies. Since the collapse of the Soviet empire, they have dismantled many of the instruments of Soviet-style bureaucracy and have made strides towards modernizing and rationalizing their public administration systems, particularly under the influence of European Union accession. Neutral competence as a principle remains precarious, however, owing in part to the rapid, parallel development of their infant democracies, a process that often results in a spoils system in the enthusiasm to take charge.

Interestingly, several of these countries are also leaping into experiments with NPM. This is also the case with other countries where there is a somewhat weak institutionalization of some of the features of traditional public administration. Some countries in Latin America fall into this category. There is a weak or imperfect notion of the value of an independent, merit-based civil service in these countries but quite aggressive adoption of elements of NPM and responsive governance models alike. More generally, there is an attraction among people concerned with economic and social development in developing countries to models of grass-roots, bottom-up responsive governance. Viet Nam might be included in this group although there is uncertainty about the effects of participative, responsive governance on party control. Nevertheless, cautious decentralization and forms of grass-roots democracy and co-production are commonplace alongside marketization initiatives.

The resilience of traditional civil service values

The ethos of public service is the most important feature of the Australian Public Service. The Committee views with alarm the perception that, with decentralization and devolution, the concept of working for the service is being diminished.[17]

As a general conclusion, it can be said that, worldwide, traditional public administration has left some very strong, persistent legacies. Civil service systems in the traditional public administration mould, where they are firmly institutionalized, are remarkably resilient in the face of wider change—perhaps not surprisingly in that they are designed deliberately to foster stability and continuity. More than that, the traditions seem to retain their relevance to some contemporary problems of governance. This resilience of traditional civil service values is reflected in the renewal of concern in many countries for the recruitment and retention of a core of more or less permanent, committed, talented individuals, a theme that is addressed throughout the present report. One argument is that they are needed to foster a distinctive culture of public service professionalism, including a strong commitment to citizen-centred values.

The public management model emphasizes the capacity of the manager to exercise hands-on autonomy and scorns many overarching bureaucratic controls as red tape. New public management takes this further by "unbundling" the unified structures and employment systems of traditional public administration and by favouring competition between multiple, autonomous providers. Most of the public sector is "just like any other business". There is nothing special about a public service career and there is nothing sacred about a unified career civil service. Senior officials can be hired from outside and employed on contract terms; central personnel agencies are largely redundant; agency managers can do their own hiring, writing labour contracts with employees that suit their separate businesses; employment should be temporary so as to maintain flexibility and respond to market conditions; and so on.

Increasingly, there has been an acknowledgement that these developments may have led to a decline in the quality, integrity and commitment or, in other words, the professionalism of the core civil service. As shown in the technical summary, these developments are certainly associated with lowered prestige of public service. The diminution of the role of the central personnel agencies, with their eye for service-wide concerns, has meant that some significant support systems for the maintenance of core civil service institutions and values have become neglected, with some potentially serious consequences. This is important since the level of professionalism of public servants has a direct impact on public service performance.

As a consequence, central agencies have refocused on integrative functions such as development of service-wide value systems, career development and talent promotion.[18] This does not necessarily mean recreating the heavy-handed controls of a completely unified career system by an all-powerful central personnel agency. Jocelyne Bourgon, the former head of the Canadian public service, argues that a "strong sense of unity" can be based on "a common mission, a common sense of purpose and common values".[19] What is important is that institutional leadership be exercised by senior officials responsible for "corporate" interests and values and that a strong framework of guidance, monitoring and supervision be in place.

The problems caused by the absence of a service-wide "corporate capacity" have been recognized in New Zealand, where NPM reforms have been in place for two decades. The initial reforms eliminated much, if not all, of the role and capacities of the central personnel agency. The State Services Commissioner in 1999 asked that he be given responsibility to develop a solution to the absence of a corporate capacity in the public service. Since then, the New Zealand public service has moved to address a wide range of service-wide HRM issues from an increasingly explicit corporate perspective.[20]

At issue, as an Australian Public Service Commissioner has put it, is the need to "integrate devolution with coherence so that we can move effectively as a whole as well as in parts".[21] In Australia, the solution adopted is a common service-wide approach to "leadership capability development", known as the "integrated leadership strategy". It has three themes: *innovation, sustainability and integrity*. The first builds on the gains of devolution and tries to extend them to collaborative, cross-agency issues; the second seeks directly to promote sustainable improvements in leadership capability through training and career support; and the third stresses the need to "uphold and promote values" through "values-based management and leadership". The Commission has placed a great deal of emphasis on ensuring that a common code of Australian Public Service values has been promulgated, disseminated and incorporated into the daily working culture of agencies.

If, however, there is a considerable degree of continuity and if old values continue to make a comeback, the final point to make is that there appears to be no possibility of turning back. The changing conditions that have created the pressures for, among other things, smaller, more disaggregated government, partnerships with NGOs, new forms of accountability and responsiveness, and the need to engage with increasingly complex networks of communication and knowledge acquisition demand new organizational and HRM responses in the public sector.

Public administration: *responsive to whom?*

The kind of professional public administration that is needed is one that acknowledges the special requirements of management in the public service. Such professional leadership emphasizes the values of integrity and accountability as well as self-discipline in accordance with a set of commonly agreed and widely understood public service values. It also places greater importance on responsiveness in public administration compared to the traditional model.

... at the expense of professionalism and prestige of the public sector

Central agencies are increasingly refocusing on integrative functions

Absence of "corporate capacity" has proven a problem in some countries adopting NPM

There is no turning back to a prior state of administration

With the state no
longer the single
locus of power,
accountability takes
on new importance
and dimensions

With the state no longer the single locus of power in society, the meaning and importance of the concept of accountability in public management have expanded considerably. Senior public officials, for example, are increasingly expected to be responsive to the needs and demands of various stakeholder groups in society. The old notion of bureaucratic insulation is gradually giving way to new and more responsive forms of governance. These demands for greater efficiency, responsiveness and integrity in the management of public affairs have also been abetted by the ICT revolution, which has allowed for the creation of new institutional forms, relationships and networks.

Table 2 identifies six forms of accountability: political, administrative, personal, professional, output and deliberative. Each one of them has its own defining features and special mechanisms for implementation. The three public administration models notably place different emphasis on these six forms of accountability. Traditional public administration, for example, prioritizes the political and administrative accountability of senior public servants, while responsive governance promotes a more all-encompassing notion of this concept, focusing particularly on personal, professional, output and deliberative accountability. Leadership in the public service under the responsive governance model will therefore make more demands on the relational, analytical and communication skills of senior officials. The public management model, on the other hand, emphasizes, in particular, the professional and output accountability of public servants vis-à-vis the citizens and other stakeholders.

Responsiveness is a
complex and arguably
conflicting notion

In the emerging governance model, the concept of "responsiveness" is increasingly becoming a key measure of accountability. Professionalism as a value is relatively non-controversial, but responsiveness is a complex and arguably a conflicting notion to incorporate into a paradigm for public sector management, which in large part is owed to the question: responsive to whom? Below, the responsiveness of the civil service to three key stakeholders—*politicians, citizens and customers*—is briefly discussed. These stakeholder groups can be

Table 2.

Six forms of accountability

Accountability	Defining features	Mechanisms	Context
Political	Democratic, external	Chains of answerability	Democratic state
Administrative	Hierarchical, legal/formal	Rules, sanctions supervision	Bureaucracy
Personal	Internal, normative	Values, ethics	All public offices/roles
Professional	Peer-oriented, expertise	Peer review, professionalism	Expert organizations
Output	Client/customer focus	NPM, self-regulation	Market, market-type mechanisms
Deliberative	Interactive, open, public	Public hearing, transparency	Public sphere

Source:
Tero Erkkilä (2004).[22]

considered to correspond to political, output and deliberative accountability referred to here above. Citizens can be further subdivided, of course, according to the groups and interests concerned.

Responsiveness to politicians

Political responsiveness of the civil service is a delicate balancing act. The convention or rule of political impartiality embodies at the same time a norm of discretion and a commitment to serve the government of the day. In the United Kingdom, the convention has always been that once objections have been voiced and taken into account, the civil servant will loyally implement the resulting decision. This is often transformed in the hands of enthusiastic governments into an expectation of partisan political loyalty come what may. In a constitutionally entrenched one-party state, this is inescapable, but even then, the sense that the civil service should enjoy a degree of autonomy in order to pursue its professional roles in both providing policy advice and administration should be retained.

Discretion and commitment may at times be at odds . . .

It is important that a civil service be both mindful of its constitutional role of loyally serving the government of the day, that is, being responsive to its demands and priorities, and jealous of preserving its integrity and its professionalism. Because of the strategic role of civil servants in maintaining state institutions over time, statutory or some other form of institutional protection may be necessary. On a day-to-day basis, a strong voice in defence of continuity and professional integrity is desirable through the institution of a central HRM agency playing a guardianship role.

. . . as well as the need for continuity and expectation of change

However, even a fully loyal, discrete and professional core civil service does not always satisfy some incumbent governments. Valid objections and difficult questions prompted by pet political schemes are often mistaken for obstructionism. There is always a lingering sense that a band of more committed partisan loyalists would do a better job. In the United States and many other presidential systems, this is institutionalized in a system of temporary top-level political appointments. In some European countries, it is recognized that many civil servants have partisan attachments, and they are given key positions when their party is in power. Subsequently, with the election of another party to office, they may be moved to less sensitive positions without losing their status as professional civil servants.

There is always a lingering sense that partisan loyalists would do a better job

In the Westminster System, however, the impartiality principle applies to all but temporary "political staffers". To the extent that the Prime Minister and other ministers have an influence on senior appointments and on reorganizing the machinery of government, there is always pressure to remould the senior echelons in the political image of the government, putting pressure on the principle of impartiality. The demands for like-mindedness and enthusiasm for achieving the government's programme may in this case dampen the propensity to ask difficult questions. In the United Kingdom, the norms of political impartiality were so well entrenched in governing traditions that departures from them have always prompted media and parliamentary discussion.

Responsiveness to citizens and customers

Civil servants can be responsive in the second sense—to the wider citizenry—in numerous ways without necessarily being engaged in a partisan political sense. This form of responsiveness involves civil servants in monitoring and filtering public opinion and the views of concerned sections of the community. It also includes an obligation to share information and demonstrate openness through consultative mechanisms with the public.

Civil servants are responsive to a wider citizenry . . .

Finally, customer responsiveness through the service provision process is an additional requirement. The mechanisms for ensuring this can be quite different from those already discussed and include customer surveys, performance indicators that reflect quality of service provision and performance management systems that reward high levels of achievement by civil servants in light of these performance measures. League tables for schools and hospitals in the United Kingdom, for example, have proved to be popular among the public.

A civil service that is responsive to outside influence in the second two senses—to citizens and customers—is not necessarily a threat to political control by a government of the day. However, reconciling these three forms of responsiveness is an emerging challenge for most governments in the new public sector environment. In the past, civil servants often used discretion and impartiality as an excuse for being secretive and impervious even in democratic societies. However, by being more open, the civil service can be the eyes and ears for ensuring smooth public input and swift feedback, and it can also act as the guarantor of consent and legitimacy through assuring quality public services.

Some civil services with a proud tradition, particularly in countries undergoing a process of democratization, may find too much political control to be threatening. The civil services in several of the high-performing Asian economies (HPAEs), which took it upon themselves to fill the political gap left by the weaknesses of political institutions and thereby developed a strong sense of direct accountability to the public for the quality of public policy outcomes, may also have to learn to live with the changing conditions under which they must sacrifice some of that political accountability role to elected politicians.

In conclusion, it can be said that the evolving management of public affairs "from government to governance" is changing accountability relationships in the public service in a major way. Some of the likely implications may include the following:

- Accountability conflicts in the public service will increase;
- Public officials will be required to exercise increasing judgement over which form of accountability to prioritize in a given circumstance;
- Professional/personal accountability will become more important for public administrators—senior administrators will have new leadership roles to play;
- Political accountability will become less dominant; and
- Political representatives will become increasingly required to assume "meta-accountability" roles—i.e., monitoring the "accountability system" for its overall results and integrity.

Towards a new synthesis

Combining and reconciling the different meanings of accountability and responsiveness, let alone the different models of public administration, reflect the challenges posed by a new synthesis of HRM practices. In some cases, traditional public administration may account for essential components of local solutions that also seek to apply NPM principles and instruments. Additionally, when the most recent innovations in the management of public sector human resources are considered (for instance, attempts to revive core public service values, build collaborative cultures and develop new forms of leadership), it is clear that some of them are a direct response to gaps and failings in NPM and even seek to resurrect, in new institutional forms, some of the principles of traditional public administration and pre-NPM professional management.

The core civil service has a more complex and demanding role to play in the model of responsive governance. Accountability must be multifaceted to be effective, and this places new demands on the discretion and professionalism of senior officials. Their leadership is essential for preserving important values of impartiality and integrity while furthering communication flows and consultative mechanisms for interaction with society. At the same time, they are charged with assuring the sound management of public service delivery in response to customer needs and entitlements. Each of these leadership functions requires a very high level of skills. Whether or not the actual service delivery is undertaken by "non-core" or non-civil service employees, the key challenge for ensuring high-capacity public administration is posed by the quality and integrity of this core group of civil servants.

The core civil service, especially senior officials, needs to pave the way

In creating an enabling environment for effective responses to the challenges facing the public sector today, leadership by dedicated professionals working in a civil service environment that provides them with both moral and material support is of paramount importance (see also chapter VI). Facing up to organizational and institutional challenges through the choice of effective, appropriate public sector development strategies is doubly challenging in developing countries because of both the urgent need to respond in the face of dire impact and a relative scarcity of resources. However, tackling these external challenges also clearly requires that effective governance structures be in place.

Leadership by dedicated professionals is of paramount importance

A new HRM synthesis should build on the best attributes of the three models. Traditional public administration, for example, is anchored in the enduring principles of impartiality and merit; public management places particular importance on performance management and professionalism; and the governance paradigm stresses the need to make public administration more responsive to the demands of citizens and other stakeholders. The present report suggests that the unifying principles of such an HRM synthesis in the public service could be *impartiality, professionalism* and *responsiveness.*

The preceding discussion has identified the components of a possible HRM synthesis as it relates to the civil service:

- A politically impartial, professional and merit-based civil service;

- A core "guardian" agency, exercising strategic leadership and monitoring a system of dispersed management rather than operating through bureaucratic controls;

- A strong focus on results-oriented management in the public service through the use of effective performance standards and indicators as well as promotion criteria giving greater weight to relative efficiency (rather than relying only on seniority);

- Tough, objective anti-corruption rules and agencies;

- Legislative provisions and professional norms that facilitate making the civil service open to external scrutiny; and

- Systems and skill sets that provide high levels of communication capacity through being networked by the effective deployment of information technology.

For this framework to produce the desired high levels of performance, especially given the kinds of challenges identified later in this report, the role of strategic human resource management, discussed in chapter V, is critical.

Notes

1   Spence, Jonathan (1969). Lay and Hart: Power, Patronage, and Pay. In *To Change China: Western Advisers in China*. New York: Little Brown.

2   Pollitt, Christopher (1990). *Managerialism and the Public Services*. Oxford: Blackwell.

3   For surveys and analysis of what constitutes NPM, see Christopher Hood (1991). A public management for all seasons? *Public Administration,* vol. 69, issue 1, pp. 3–19; and Martin Minogue (1999). Changing the state: concepts and practices in the reform of the public sector. In *Beyond the New Public Management: Changing Ideas and Practices in Governance,* M. Minogue, C. Polidano and D. Hulme, eds. Cheltenham: Edward Elgar.

4   This distinction is made by Nick Manning (2001). The legacy of the new public management in developing countries. *International Review of Administrative Science*, vol. 67, issue 2, pp. 297–312.

5   Among them David Osborne and Ted Gaebler (1992). *Reinventing Government: How the Entrepreneurial Spirit Is Transforming the Public Sector*. Reading, MA: Addison Wesley Publishing Company.

6   Boston, Jonathon, John Martin, June Pallott and Pat Walsh (1996). *Public Management: the New Zealand Model*. Auckland: Oxford University Press.

7   Hood, Christopher (2000). Relations between ministers/politicians and public servants. In *Governance in the Twenty-first Century: Revitalizing the Public Service*, B. Guy Peters and Donald J. Savoie, eds. Montreal and Kingston: McGill-Queens University Press; also Christoph Knill (1999). Explaining cross-national variance in administrative reform: autonomous versus instrumental bureaucracies. *Journal of Public Policy*, vol. 19, issue 2, pp.113–139; and Michio Muramatsu and Frieder Naschold (1997). Future perspectives of state and administration in Japan and Germany. In *State and Administration in Japan and Germany*, Michio Muramatsu and Frieder Naschold, eds. Berlin: Walter de Gruyter.

8   This has long been the practice in Sweden. As usual, something claimed to be "new" can always be found in a previously unremarked precedent. The distinctiveness of the NPM model lies in the combination of this with other features under the banner of a comprehensive, inclusive doctrine.

9   Moore, Mark H. (1995). *Creating Public Value: Strategic Management in Government*. Cambridge, MA: Harvard University Press.

10   World Bank (1994). *Governance: the World Bank's Experience*. Washington, D.C.: World Bank; and David Williams and Tom Young (1994). Governance, the World Bank and liberal theory. *Political Studies*, vol. 42, issue 1, pp. 84–100.

11   World Bank (2000). Broadening our approach: empowering our clients and fostering accountability. In *Reforming Public Institutions and Strengthening Governance*. Washington, D.C.: World Bank.

12   For discussions of governance theory, see Jon Pierre, ed. (2000). *Debating Governance: Authority, Steering, and Democracy*. Oxford: Oxford University Press.

13   Behn, Robert (2001). *Rethinking Democratic Accountability*. Washington, D.C.: Brookings Institution Press.

14   The *World Public Sector Report 2003: E-Government at the Crossroads* also dealt extensively with the use of ICTs in government.

15   For a survey, see Christopher Pollitt and Geert Bouckaert (2000). *Public Management Reform: A Comparative Analysis*. Oxford: Oxford University Press.

16   See, for example, United Nations (2003). *World Public Sector Report 2003: E-Government at the Crossroads*. Department of Economic and Social Affairs. Sales No. E.03.II.H.3.

17   Australian Joint Committee of Public Accounts. In Alan Lawton (1998). *Ethical Management for the Public Services*. Buckingham, United Kingdom: Open University Press.

18   Aucoin, Peter and Herman Bakvis (2004). Public service reform and policy capacity: recruiting and retaining the best and the brightest? In *Challenges to State Policy Capacity*, Martin Painter and Jon Pierre, eds. Basingstoke: Palgrave MacMillan.

19   Bourgon, Jocelyne (2002). A unified public service: does it matter? Paper at CPAM Biennial Conference. Glasgow, 11 September.

20   Government of New Zealand (1999). Briefing for the Minister of State Services. State Services
Commission. 10 December; and Government of New Zealand (2002). The review from the
centre—one year on: getting better results for citizens, ministers and staff. State Services
Commission (December). Available from http://www.ssc.govt.nz/upload/downloadable_files/
roc-one-year-on.pdf

21   See, for example, the case of Australia described by Andrew S. Podger (2004). Innovation with
integrity—the public sector leadership imperative to 2020. *Australian Journal of Public
Administration*, vol. 63, issue 1 (March), pp. 11–21.

22   Erkkilä, Tero (2004). Governance and accountability—a shift in conceptualisation? EGPA 2004
Annual Conference. Ljubljana, Slovenia, 1–4 September. Available from http://www.fu.uni-lj.si/
egpa2004/html/sg7/Erkkila.pdf

Chapter II
Human resource management and government performance

Why HRM matters

The importance of merit-oriented HRM policies

Fundamentally, man is the key to all problems, not money. Funds are valuable only when used by trained, experienced and devoted men and women. Such people, on the other hand, can work miracles even with small resources and draw wealth out of barren land.

—Dag Hammarskjöld[1]

The present chapter is divided into three main parts. It begins with a discussion of why the quality of HRM in the public sector is so critical for government performance and national development. It then emphasizes that governments need to embark on HRM reform from where they find themselves by laying solid foundations before moving on to more complex initiatives. Finally, the chapter highlights the importance of both political commitment and political feasibility for the success of HRM reform in the public sector.

The lessons learned from the "lost decade" of the 1980s in many developing countries, particularly in Africa and Latin America, with its emphasis on downsizing and structural adjustment policies, demonstrate that the promotion of economic growth and poverty reduction is not associated with the weakening of government institutions, but quite the contrary. More recently, the same can be said of the experiences of many transition economies during the 1990s. The *World Public Sector Report 2001* concluded that countries successful in reaping the benefits of globalization were generally those with the most developed and comprehensive public sectors.[2]

These lessons are reflected in a number of studies within the last ten years that have converged on the significance of efficient management of human resources in enhancing government performance and national development. Focusing primarily on developing countries, the studies have in turn suggested that specific structural features of state bureaucracies enhance economic growth, facilitate government performance and reduce poverty. In this section, we will briefly examine the key findings and conclusions of some of these studies as well other related insights from the private sector.

Linear multiple regression analysis applied to cross-country data by UN/DESA has measured the impact of selected variables on the quality and integrity of the public service and the prestige of public sector employment (box 2). The analysis confirms a positive correlation between merit-based recruitment as well as promotion and the quality as well as integrity of the public service, but not the prestige of public sector employment. Better remuneration of senior officials also increases the quality and integrity of bureaucracies and enhances the prestige of public sector employment outside Africa.

Reforms in the 1980s and 1990s often undermined state capacities, yet . . .

. . . development is not associated with the weakening of government institutions

Efficient HRM enhances government performance and national development

Box 2

UN/DESA analysis of government performance

The findings of statistical analysis performed by UN/DESA largely corroborate the conclusions of earlier studies in this area, namely, that the quality of human resource management has a significant impact on the performance of government institutions. The sources of data for the UN/DESA analysis were surveys of expert opinion from the International Country Risk Guide (between 97 and 140 countries), the State Capacity Survey (between 97 and 129 countries) and a survey first carried out for 35 countries by James E. Rauch and Peter Evans and later extended by the United Nations University (UNU) to cover an additional 16 African countries. In the UN/DESA analysis, the Rauch and Evans and the UNU datasets were consolidated into one.

The following are selected findings of the UN/DESA analysis:

Professionalism in the civil service is an excellent predictor of both the quality and the integrity of the public service, and its effects are consistently positive. The results from surveys of 121 countries illustrate this relationship:

Scatter plot 1.
Bureaucratic quality and merit

Scatter plot 2.
Integrity and merit

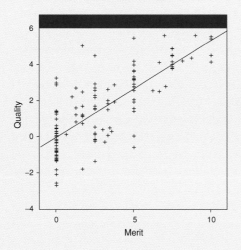

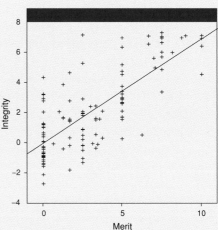

Source: UN/DESA.

Note: Plot of quality against merit in 1999 (121 countries), controlling for selected variables.

Source: UN/DESA.

Note: Plot of integrity against merit in 1999 (121 countries), controlling for selected variables.

Legal remuneration (salary plus perquisites) of senior public officials relative to their counterparts in the private sector has some positive effect on bureaucratic quality and a much stronger positive effect on integrity, whereas, notably, *extra-legal remuneration* (tips and bribes) has no significant effect on the quality of bureaucracy in the public sector.

New public management (NPM), measured indirectly as mobility of high-level personnel between the public and private sectors, is not a significant determinant of the quality or the integrity of the civil service. NPM, on the other hand, is a significant negative determinant of the prestige of a public sector career for recent university graduates, but weaker and less significant for African than for non-African countries.

Source:
See "Technical summary".

The UN/DESA analysis relied partly on two well-known earlier studies based on a survey of expert opinions on the quality of state bureaucracies in 35 developing countries.[3] The first study came to the conclusion that state bureaucracies with meritocratic recruitment and predictable as well as rewarding long-term careers were generally associated with superior economic growth. The second one found that the single most important element in improving bureaucratic performance is meritocratic recruitment. It asserted that the institutionalization of meritocratic recruitment in developing countries is crucial to ensure that performance benefits will outlast pressures of the moment. The study also emphasized the importance of promotion from within and career stability, ultimately suggesting that the behaviour of bureaucrats is rooted in organizational norms and structures.

These two studies were later complemented by a United Nations University (UNU) survey that added 16 African countries to the sample.[4] The UNU study concluded that public agencies do better, provide better services and are less corrupt and more responsive to private sector concerns if the staff they employ are paid well and have access to internal promotion not distorted by patronage and if they have a decent degree of autonomy from the centre of government.

A more recent study examined the relationship between the capacity of state bureaucracies and poverty reduction.[5] Using data from the two surveys mentioned earlier, the study included 29 developing and middle-income countries. It concluded that there is indeed a strong relationship between states with competent and effective public institutions and their ability to reduce poverty.

The *1997 World Development Report* also drew attention to the contemporary conditions in which states function. A couple of years later, the World Bank constructed an index for "government effectiveness", comprising the quality of public bureaucracy, policy-making and service delivery, as one of six elements of a measure of governance.[6] When government effectiveness was tested against data from 175 countries, the analysis confirmed not only the close link with economic growth in the above-mentioned studies but also that government effectiveness contributed to higher national income.[7] Moreover, business people in the developing and transitional countries surveyed ranked government effectiveness ahead of economic factors such as high inflation and exchange rate regime distortions and only behind control of corruption in terms of importance to business success.

In addition, there also exists a large group of robust studies of private companies, initially in industrialized countries but more recently in developing countries and transition economies as well, that support the bureaucracy studies by demonstrating that the quality of firms' management of human resources is closely related to their overall performance. As a result, effective management of human resources in the private sector is increasingly recognized as an important source of competitive advantage, partly because so few firms use it properly, unlike new technology, for example, on which every self-respecting company spends money.

There is also solid evidence that HRM is not simply connected with organizational performance but actually determines it.[8] While the evidence that human resources have an impact on a firm's performance is impressive and continues to grow, more precise information is still lacking about which human resource practices have the greatest impact. One leading scholar has highlighted the following practices for their effects on the performance of firms: selective recruitment, remuneration contingent on performance, training, reduction in status differentials, sharing information, self-managing teams and employment security.[9]

There is also evidence that it is as much the way an organization aligns different practices in a strategic architecture as individual actions that have an impact: synergy means

Margin notes

Economic growth is associated with a merit-based bureaucracy

Bureaucracies perform better if staff are professional and well-paid

Competent and effective institutions facilitate poverty reduction

Government effectiveness is one cause of higher economic growth

HRM is increasingly recognized as a source of competitive advantage

HRM is a determinant of organizational performance

HRM is subject to
national and sectoral
differences

that the whole may be greater than the sum of the parts. Moreover, while there is some evidence that practices such as those listed above are transferable to non-Western and non-English-speaking countries, the "contingency" tradition in management thinking shows that the parts themselves may differ somewhat from place to place. Pay contingent on performance, for example, is notoriously subject to national and sectoral differences, as discussed in chapter V.

In conclusion, it is important to note that effective institutions do not exist in a vacuum. Yet in the traditional notion of bureaucracy, the relationship between the bureaucracy and the external world, its environment, is not given any prominence. Autonomy from societal interference is not, however, sufficient for institutions to become effective and spur socio-economic development. An important lesson learned is that "bureaucracies need to become embedded in concrete social ties that bind them together".[10] Furthermore, governments in both developed and developing countries need to strike a fine balance between strengthening *bureaucratic autonomy* and fostering the *societal embeddedness* of civil servants. Embeddedness in this context signifies that governments have put in place institutional channels for regular consultation and negotiation of objectives and priorities with various groups in society.

Attaining a fine balance between bureaucratic autonomy and societal embeddedness is a real challenge for any public administration and requires a high level of leadership skills, as discussed later in this report. An aloof and unapproachable bureaucracy, out of touch with reality, is as undesirable as an administration presiding over a spoils system. The challenge, therefore, is to develop a public service that is *impartial* and *professional*, but also *responsive* to civil society and business, while being neither populist nor captured by special interests. The experiences of a number of Latin American countries as well as some of the recently industrialized states in East Asia show just how difficult this can be.

Government as a "model employer"

In part because of the findings discussed earlier, governments are gradually changing the importance attributed to HRM in public sector management. Governments are realizing that managing staff in the public sector is one of the most powerful yet least appreciated ways to achieve their political and strategic objectives. Some are also becoming more cognizant of their special responsibility to act as a "model employer" in society. Governments are generally the largest employer in the labour market, which adds to their responsibility of being a conscientious employer and to "raising the bar" when it comes to HRM, for example, by promoting measures such as the following:

- Optimizing conditions for staff to develop;
- Preserving the dignity of employees, particularly their right to participate in decisions that affect them; and
- Ensuring that the talents of all the groups from which the public workforce is drawn, both women and men, members of various ethnic groups and so on, are effectively harnessed.

Allocation of resources
is only one side of
the HR coin

These issues will be further discussed in subsequent chapters of the report. However, it should not be forgotten in this context that governments, even in poor countries, regularly spend substantial resources on the development of their staff through centrally funded institutes of public administration as well as other capacity-building programmes.

Nevertheless, the same governments often fail to obtain adequate return on investments in training and capacity development since the skills that staff have acquired at public expense are not used to the fullest extent in many instances. At the same time, managers are sometimes frustrated that staff do not contribute fully to the work of their agencies. These divergent views highlight the need to strengthen dialogue between management and staff on both performance expectations and capacity development strategies in the public sector.

Dialogue on performance expectations facilitates better utilzation of resources

HRM reform: *"starting from where you find yourself"*

The preceding discussion has provided both performance-related and ethical arguments as to why the quality of HRM in the public sector should be a central concern of governments. The apparent question is: what strategy should governments follow when it comes to HRM reform? The main message of the report is that the content and sequencing of HRM reform will depend on the pre-existing structure of public administration in a given country. For example, with the formal decolonization of Africa, Asia and Latin America now almost complete and the consequences of the break-up of the Soviet Union having been worked through, there have been only exceptional cases in recent years where a government has had the luxury of turning over a new leaf (Timor-Leste is one). Even South Africa's first majority rule government, which in many respects represented a clean break with a history of public administration based on skin colour, continued with existing government structures, such as the ministry responsible for managing the civil service, after the handover of power.

Pre-existing structures of public administration should guide HRM reform

Like South Africa, most, if not all, countries have put in place a legal and institutional framework to manage the public service. However imperfect these laws and institutions may be, they have usually developed through custom and practice, and the public servants, whose behaviour they govern, have become used to them. Thus, governments are well advised to start—and virtually always do—from where they find themselves, developing and adjusting gradually to meet the requirements of the day rather than attempting an HRM "year zero" with some blueprint model drawn from an international "best practice".

Governments are well advised to start from where they find themselves

It is this "path-dependent" character of public service institutions and procedures—the result of their history—at least as much as cultural differences that explains why governments vary to such an extent in the basic structures that they have put in place to manage staff. In some cases, though, carefully planning for contingencies may enable governments to get both the "mix" and the "sequencing" right (see chapter IV). Yet it is worthwhile keeping in mind Edward Said's lapidary phrase: "History cannot be swept clean like a blackboard".[11]

The United Nations Committee of Experts on Public Administration was one of the early advocates of this viewpoint, which has more recently been highlighted in the *World Development Report 2004*. While some countries need to lay the foundations for HRM by putting into place the necessary legal and regulatory framework and ensuring that these policies are being followed, other countries, where the foundations are strong, already have the luxury of building on them, for example by delegating authority to line managers. To illustrate this point, table 3 presents a two-stage model of HRM reform, with different approaches for each stage.

These findings suggest that, at the early stages of reform, governments would be well advised to focus their efforts, whenever possible, on institutionalizing a unified, merit-oriented career civil service before embarking on more complex initiatives, such as devolution of HRM and introduction of a position-based system. The model also recognizes that countries at different stages of public sector development may move in opposite directions at different

Before embarking on complex reform initiatives, a solid foundation should be in place

Table 3.
Approaches for different stages of HRM reform

Objective	First-stage reform	Second-stage reform
Career management	Enhance job security and protection from political interference	Create a core civil service; introduce 360-degree accountability to stakeholders
Unity of the civil service civil service	Create a legally defined cadre with common terms and conditions	Central regulation of HRM; decentralized HRM; pay flexibility
Individual incentives	Consistently apply standard merit promotion and reward rules	Greater use of performance criteria in promotion and rewards
Openness	Encourage career development within a closed system and avoid nepotism	Both vertical and lateral entry into core career service

Source:
Adapted from
World Bank (2004).[12]

times but still achieve the same policy objectives. Thus, some governments, such as in the Republic of Korea and Sri Lanka, have retained or strengthened central control over staffing as a priority, while other countries, such as Finland and New Zealand, have taken steps to reduce it. In staffing as in other kinds of reform, "vice may be virtue uprooted".[13]

Reform requires sound political diagnosis

Political leadership
is needed to see
reform through

Acknowledging pre-existing structures of public administration may be a necessary condition for successful reform, yet it is not sufficient. Political leadership is every bit as important in public administration reform as it is in other areas of reform. However, in order for leadership to be exercised, political leaders must assess the feasibility of reform before actually committing themselves. Benin's experience, in particular the role played by its former President, Nicéphore Soglo, shows how the better part of a leader's valour can be discretion (box 3).

Contrary to the experience of Benin, the Government of Uganda was able to push through reform largely based on World Bank policies because of greater stakeholder support. These experiences highlight that political acumen and judgement are important qualities of leaders in the public sector who are embarking on difficult reforms.

Assessing the feasibility of reform does not mean giving up, ruling out opportunities to improve the way that staff work and/or are managed simply because they are politically difficult. It helps to have a clear sense of the stakeholders involved and to use standard organizational change techniques, as presented in figure 1. This figure is based on the recent experience of Morocco, a country struggling to reform its staffing at the time of the study on which the figure is based. It uses the well-known force field analysis technique from the armoury of organizational change practices to show the forces that supported and opposed reform in Morocco. Such an analysis may appear mechanical on paper, but in real life, it requires sensitivity, suppleness and judgement.

Box 3

Political discretion in reform—Benin

President Soglo, despite sharing the World Bank's policies as its former Regional Director, could not stick to that ideology as a politician. He received much praise in the 1990s when he was Prime Minister for managing to pay the country's 47,000 civil servants regularly and even paying some salary arrears as well as convicting some leaders who had been involved in financial scandals.

However, when President Soglo tried to implement fundamental staffing reform with austerity measures, he met with stiff opposition from the unions and Members of Parliament. His situation was made worse by the 1994 massive devaluation of the CFA franc ... While the President was stressing "good economics" some of his adversaries were stressing "good socio-political elements". The defeat of Soglo in the election, which followed in 1996, and subsequent elections would tend to show that the socio-political pressures had leverage on the voters. It would seem that political forces were sceptical about his structural adjustment policies and the transformation envisaged towards the existing system, including the civil service.

One of the messages from the Benin experience is that it is unwise to collapse the issues of political feasibility into a simple formula of "political will". In other words, President Soglo's personal commitment to World Bank-style staffing reform was not enough to make the programme survive when the strain on the political system became too great. His vision for reform was not shared by other key stakeholders in the political establishment. Benin in the 1990s was one of those cases where political feasibility rather than political commitment or will was lacking, given the character of the main stakeholder groups whose acquiescence government needed to obtain.

Sources:
See Bibliography.

Morocco's experience shows that an HRM reform could succeed even where others have previously failed if officials give ministers a feasible proposal that takes account of what stakeholders will countenance while sacrificing as little as possible of the essence of reform. It bears out the observation made by one influential international organization that "in many respects, political will is a function of the quality of advice provided (by officials) to politicians".[14]

Political will is often a function of the quality of advice provided to politicians

Figure 1.
Driving and restraining forces in Moroccan reform

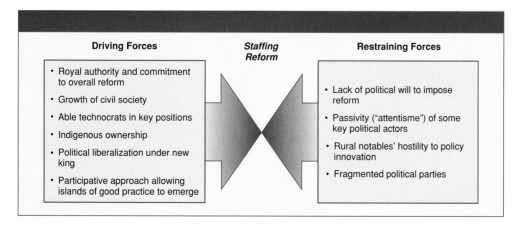

Driving Forces	Staffing Reform	Restraining Forces
• Royal authority and commitment to overall reform • Growth of civil society • Able technocrats in key positions • Indigenous ownership • Political liberalization under new king • Participative approach allowing islands of good practice to emerge		• Lack of political will to impose reform • Passivity ("attentisme") of some key political actors • Rural notables' hostility to policy innovation • Fragmented political parties

Source:
Adapted from Al-Arkoubi and McCourt (2004).[15]

Leadership commitment is necessary

Staffing reform that will improve government effectiveness, such as Sri Lanka's constitutional amendment in 2001 to re-establish an independent Public Service Commission, requires the commitment of both politicians and senior officials. Even when allowance is made for programmes that were never feasible in the first place, an analysis showing that lack of political commitment was the biggest single explanation for the failure of around 40 per cent of civil service reform projects of the World Bank in the mid-1990s should not be discounted.[16]

A study of staffing reform in Swaziland has revealed that when a given reform is feasible and the antecedents of reform are adequate, leaders may choose to make a realistic commitment that can be expected to lead to concrete reform. Antecedents of reform in this case are comprised of political capability (e.g., strong political base and leadership) and administrative capacity (e.g., united reform team and overall capacity). Reform will be binding to the extent that it is:

- *Voluntary* (not imposed by a donor or other outside agent against the government's better judgement);

- *Explicit* (clear and straightforward, not hedged with qualifications or riders);

- *Challenging* (it will lead to substantial, not trivial, improvements);

- *Public* (leaders have publicized their commitment in the mass media and in other ways); and

- *Irrevocable* (leaders have not allowed themselves an easy line of retreat if conditions become difficult).

What increases commitment? The first step is to analyse the politics of staffing reform: governments can deal only with factors of which they are aware. Identifying reform stakeholders and conducting a force field analysis, as outlined above, are two possible methods in this regard. This is important because the factors that increase commitment are specific to every situation since they are rooted in the politics of a particular country.

Governments will consequently proceed in ways that make political sense to them. To take one example, the Swaziland study suggested that the Government needed to distinguish between its fundamental interest in the continuation of the monarchical political system and its contingent interest in perpetuating a system of patron-client relations in the allocation of government jobs. It pointed to the need to restore the independence of the Civil Service Board, the body responsible for civil service staffing, as an "irrevocable" step that would demonstrate the Government's commitment to reform.

The question of commitment matters only when the programme that a leader is expected to spearhead is challenging and has powerful opponents so that the possibility of failure and ignominy is real. No particular vision, for example, is generally needed to implement an innocuous policy such as a pay rise for public servants. Even where reform is feasible and where policy-makers have decided to commit themselves to it, leadership is still needed to see it through. While countries successful in strengthening public administration have pursued different reform strategies, they have all had in common leadership that possessed the capacity to make difficult decisions and implement them.

The experience of reform furthermore shows that successful leaders are hands-on; leadership can be delegated only up to a point. In Malaysia, for example, Prime Minister Mahathir personally chaired all ten meetings of the committee that reformed Malaysia's civil service pay and introduced performance appraisal with a performance pay element.[17] Ten years later, it was his personal initiative that caused radical amendments to that same appraisal scheme in response to complaints from the civil servants' trade union about unfair subjectivity in the way that it operated. In the United Kingdom, Prime Minister Thatcher's well-known staffing reforms in the 1980s were not very different from those of her predecessor, Harold Wilson, in the 1960s. What was different was that she gave them quality time and followed them through to full implementation.

Successful leaders are hands-on

Notes

1 Hammarskjöld, Dag, former Secretary-General, United Nations. In United Nations (1995). Human Resources Development. Twelfth Meeting of Experts on the United Nations Programme in Public Administration and Finance. ST/SG/AC.6/1995/L.7/Add.1.

2 United Nations (2001). *World Public Sector Report: Globalization and the State*. Department of Economic and Social Affairs. Sales No. E.01.II.H.2.

3 Evans, Peter and James E. Rauch (1999). Bureaucracy and growth: a cross-national analysis of the effects of "Weberian" state structures on economic growth. *American Sociological Review*, vol. 64, no. 5 (October) and Rauch, James E. and Peter Evans (2000). Bureaucratic structure and bureaucratic performance in less developed countries. *Journal of Public Economics*, vol. 75, No. 1 (January), pp. 49–71.

4 Court, Julius, Petra Kristen and Beatrice Weder (1999). Bureaucratic structure and performance: first Africa survey results (draft of 20 December). Available from http://www.unu.edu/hq/academic/Pg_area4/pdf/unu-research.pdf

5 Henderson, Jeffrey and others (2003). *Bureaucratic Effects: "Weberian" State Structures and Poverty Reduction*. Working Paper No. 31. Chronic Poverty Research Center. Available from http://www.chronicpoverty.org/cpreports2.htm

6 Kaufmann, Daniel, Aart Kray and Massimo Mastruzzi (2003). Governance Matters III: Governance Indicators for 1996–2002. Washington, D.C.: World Bank.

7 Kaufmann, Daniel (1999). Governance redux: the empirical challenge. In *The Global Competitiveness Report 2003–2004*, Michal E. Porter and others. World Economic Forum. New York and Oxford: Oxford University Press.

8 Becker, Brian and Barry Gerhart (1996). The impact of human resource management on organizational performance: progress and prospects. *Academy of Management Journal*, vol. 39, No. 4 (August), pp. 779–801; and M. Patterson, M. West, R. Lawthorn and S. Nickell (1997). The impact of people management practices on business performance. *Issues in People Management*, No. 22. London: Institute of Personnel and Development.

9 Pfeffer, Jeffrey (1998). *The Human Equation: Building Profits by Putting People First*. Boston, MA: Harvard Business School.

10 Form, William (1997). Embedded autonomy: states and industrial transformation. *Administrative Science Quarterly*, vol. 42, no. 1, pp. 187–189.

11 Said, Edward (1978). *Orientalism*. New York: Random House.

12 World Bank (2004). *World Development Report 2004: Making Services Work for Poor People*. Washington D.C.: World Bank.

13 Jones, David (1974). The tribune's visitation. In *The Sleeping Lord and Other Fragments*, David Jones. London: Faber and Faber, pp. 42–58.

14 World Bank (1998). *Public Expenditure Management Handbook*. Poverty and Social Policy Department. Washington, D.C.: World Bank. Available from http://www1.worldbank.org/publicsector/pe/handbook/pem98.pdf

15 Al-Arkoubi, K. and Willy McCourt (2004). The politics of HRM: waiting for Godot in the Moroccan civil service. *International Journal of Human Resource Management*, vol. 15, issue 6.

16 Nunberg, Barbara (1997). *Rethinking Civil Service Reform: An Agenda for Smart Government*. Poverty and Social Policy Working Paper. Washington, D.C.: World Bank.

17 Government of Malaysia (1991). *Report of the Special Committee of the Cabinet on Salaries for the Public Sector*. Kuala Lumpur: National Printing Department.

Chapter III
Socio-economic challenges facing HRM

Major socio-economic challenges are confronting governments and posing serious questions about the sustainability and integrity of key aspects of public sector human resource systems. Prominent among those challenges with a direct impact on human resource management are demographic shifts; trends in labour migration, including the so-called "brain drain"; and the impact of HIV/AIDS on labour markets and public services, especially in sub-Saharan Africa. These challenges bring unanticipated shocks with unexpected spillover effects for the public sector, including the management of human resources.

The economic and social processes that underlie these challenges may, in turn, be affected by policy responses, but such is the interconnectedness of nation states in the global system that some of these responses may, in turn, produce unanticipated adverse effects on other countries. Such processes highlight the need for all governments to acquire greater policy-making capacity through more strategic husbanding, upgrading and deployment of scarce human skills and the knowledge systems that human resources manage.

A common thread running through these socio-economic challenges is that they affect in some measure both developed and developing countries. However, their most severe impact is experienced by poor countries in their continuing struggle for human development and poverty reduction. This struggle is starkly manifested in many poor countries by a shortage of all those key resources that are necessary for effective governance—human, financial, institutional, organizational and technological.

Demographic shifts, labour migration and HIV/AIDS all pose major challenges . . .

. . . that often transcend national boundaries . . .

. . . and affect both developed and developing countries

Demographic changes

Populations all over the world are ageing. While in 1950 roughly half of the world population was older than 23 years, it is projected that by 2050, half of the population will be concentrated above the age of 36 years.[1] However, this phenomenon has vastly different causes and implications for different parts of the world.

Thus, the increasing number of old people in the population in places such as India is largely the result of improved health and a higher life expectancy. With declining infant mortality and a relatively high fertility rate, the number of young people entering the workforce continues to grow—the working-age population is growing faster than the general population, a trend that is the reverse of that prevailing in the developed countries.[2]

In Europe and Japan, by contrast, longer life expectancy is accompanied by a rapid decline in the birth rate as patterns of family life and child-rearing change, resulting in an increasingly smaller workforce and an inversion of the classic population pyramid. Considering that a fertility rate of 2.1 is the replacement rate, Italy's fertility rate has declined to 1.2, Germany's to 1.3 and Japan's to 1.4.[3] In these countries, the very low employee-to-retiree ratios that will be faced in the very near future pose serious problems of equity and sustainability for state welfare and fiscal systems.

China is an example of a developing country that has experienced declining fertility rates—in this case as a result of consistent government policy. Combined with increasing longevity, China's ageing population is posing a major challenge for the government in the years to come (box 4).

The world population is ageing rapidly

Box 4

Old age, new challenges—China

China is facing new challenges as the result of an ageing workforce. This situation is triggered by two fundamental demographics: a declining fertility rate and increasing longevity. Furthermore, considering that state employees are generally both older and ageing at a more rapid pace than their private-sector counterparts, this issue is becoming a major HRM challenge. First, the demand for skilled employees continues to grow, and the public sector faces fiercer competition with the private sector for talent. Second, the increased number of retirees in the public sector will deprive the Government of valuable institutional memory. Those aged 60 and above will make up 30 per cent of the Chinese population by the year 2050 (see figures). Recognizing the potential implications of an ageing workforce for the civil service, the Government has initiated specific strategies to address this emerging situation.

Population pyramid of China, 2000

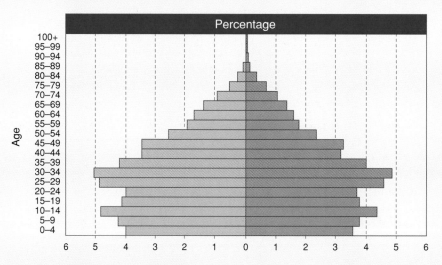

Population pyramid of China, 2050

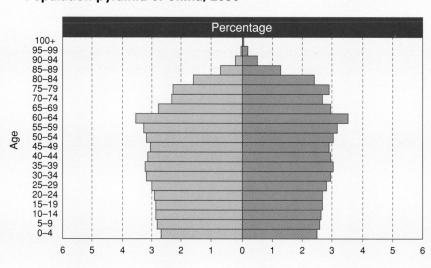

Source:
United Nations (2003).

Note:
Calculations based on medium variant projections.

Box 4 (cont'd)

Recruitment

As an important first step, the Government has revised its recruitment system for civil servants. Based on analysis of future staffing needs, the Ministry of Personnel recently introduced the Temporary Act for Civil Servants, which includes a strategic recruitment plan to address challenges posed by the ageing workforce. In addition to academic credentials, work experience and skills of candidates, the Government will now pay more attention to its long-term human resources plan based on workforce, demographic and workload analysis. Candidates selected for civil service employment will also enjoy greater flexibility in choosing jobs in state agencies. This two-way recruitment system not only helps potential employees identifying the positions that best fit their own career plans but also allows the Government to find the most suitable talent for its future staffing needs.

The Government has also been making significant efforts to cultivate the loyalty of civil servants to the long-term interests of the state. Integral to this strategy has been the establishment of a career-based civil service. A number of effective practices have also been initiated aimed at enhancing the morale of civil servants through creative advertising and agency induction programmes; more diversified assignments and projects to maintain the interest of staff; revision of the incentive system to promote more flexible working arrangements, competitive salary packages, career development programmes and recognition schemes; and improvements in the promotion system to ensure that outstanding young staff have better opportunities to be considered for high-level posts.

Retraining

China's Tenth Five-Year Plan for National Economic and Social Development regards improved HRM in the public sector as one of the nation's major goals. For the first time, the Chinese Communist Party and the Government are giving top priority to the cultivation of more capable civil servants. Government agencies at all levels are required to develop training programmes to improve the competencies of public servants in order to avoid potential knowledge gaps in the future. One innovation is the Masters in Public Administration (MPA) Programme that targets young talent in the public service. Moreover, most training programmes are integrated with international practices, and advanced theories and experiences from developed countries are widely studied. Another innovative practice is e-training that takes advantage of advanced technology to leverage the potential of knowledge management. With the rapid development of computer networks and wider application of sophisticated software, the Government intends to develop mechanisms for maintaining its institutional memory and to distribute knowledge more widely across organizational boundaries.

Replacement

Repair your roof before rain! This old Chinese saying has a new meaning today. To prepare for the imminent retirement wave, the Government has launched succession management programmes within the public sector. Systematic efforts have been made to analyse public-sector workforce trends, project future human resource needs, identify potential candidates for future vacancies, and develop diversified competencies through various training programmes. Both central and local governments have also started to accelerate the development of talent pools. Those with very strong potential are even offered temporary leadership positions in local governments and other agencies to improve their competencies for future assignments.

Sources:
See Bibliography.

The impact of an ageing population on human resource policy and practices in the public sector can be significant, but the effects vary according to the circumstances of different countries. In Europe, a post-war expansion of governments, which created a "baby-boom bulge" in the age profile of some public services, was recently accentuated by the fact that since the 1980s, the rate of recruitment of new public servants to the lower grades has slowed down

For many countries, recruitment has followed a downward trend since the 1980s as governments have downsized. As a result, in OECD countries, the proportion of civil servants aged forty and over increased from 42 to 60 per cent between 1995 and 2001.[4]

Pension liabilities pose an increasing problem

One of the most difficult problems as a result of these developments is the high cost of sustaining public service pension funds and the need for reform of traditionally generous public service pension systems. Over the next five to ten years, there will be a high retirement rate, especially in OECD countries, putting a strain on pension funds (some of which may carry unfunded liabilities) and increasing the demand on employees to help to fund these pensions. In spite of political costs, governments may be forced to reduce their retirement benefits by, for example, raising the age of retirement.

More pensioners than actual staff in Brazil's civil service

Where the pension fund carries very heavy unfunded liabilities and the benefits are very generous, as was the case in the pay-as-you-go (PAYG) system in Brazil (box 5), the resulting fiscal crisis can affect state finances as a whole and, as a consequence, severely constrain recruitment and remuneration policies for the civil service. Since 2000, Brazil has had more retirees and pensioners than actual employees in the civil service, and under the original pension scheme, public servants could retire on full pay after twenty-five years of service. A reform plan was approved by Congress in 2003.

Additional problems arise from ageing public services. For example, in Australia, the top-heavy age distribution of the Senior Executive Service (SES) and the expected high departure rate in the next few years as the members of this group all reach retirement age together have prompted a new set of succession-planning measures, such as greater attention to

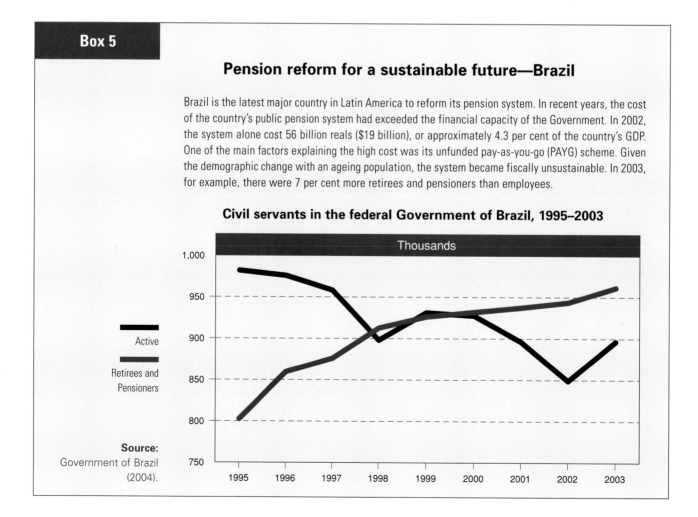

Box 5

Pension reform for a sustainable future—Brazil

Brazil is the latest major country in Latin America to reform its pension system. In recent years, the cost of the country's public pension system had exceeded the financial capacity of the Government. In 2002, the system alone cost 56 billion reals ($19 billion), or approximately 4.3 per cent of the country's GDP. One of the main factors explaining the high cost was its unfunded pay-as-you-go (PAYG) scheme. Given the demographic change with an ageing population, the system became fiscally unsustainable. In 2003, for example, there were 7 per cent more retirees and pensioners than employees.

Civil servants in the federal Government of Brazil, 1995–2003

Thousands

Active

Retirees and Pensioners

Source:
Government of Brazil
(2004).

Box 5 (cont'd)

Another factor was the generosity of the system. Before the reform, civil servants could retire after 25 years of public service, with full salary plus any subsequent pay raise given to their replacements. In 2002, about half of the country's total pension expenditure was paid to former civil servants, who accounted for only 5 per cent of the total number of retirees. The fiscal deficit caused by these high costs, therefore, deprived the Government of chances to improve the remuneration of existing staff and limited its ability to invest in training and capacity development.

A reform plan was approved by Congress in 2003, with the aim of bringing pension benefits in the public service in line with those offered in the private sector. The main goal of the reform is to lower the fiscal deficit and reduce pension inequalities across sectors. The retirement age in the civil service was raised to 60 years for men and 55 for women, which was to be phased in over 7 years. Retirees in the public service will also have to pay income taxes on their pensions as do staff in other sectors. Caps on benefits have also been introduced under the new plan. People who desire higher pension benefits will have to contribute separately to a private pension scheme. However, the changes will not hurt those already retired, whose "acquired rights" will continue to be respected.

Despite strong resistance from public sector unions, the general public has supported the pension reform in Brazil. The Government expects to reduce its pension obligations by approximately $18 billion over the next two decades as the result of this initiative. The savings will provide the Government with more resources to promote knowledge transfer, workforce planning and succession management in the public sector. The reform will also promote intergenerational equity by linking the retirement benefits of public servants to their contributions to the system rather than follow the PAYG scheme. The new reform plan also reduces the current preferential pension status of public servants vis-à-vis private sector employees. On the other hand, the pension reform may negatively impact the morale of public servants and make the public service less attractive for young talent. This will pose a challenge to the Government of Brazil as it continues to improve human resource management in the public sector.

Sources:
See Bibliography.

upgrading the skills and increasing the promotion opportunities among members of the "feeder" grades, from which most future members of the SES will be recruited.[5] Lateral recruitment from outside the civil service will also contribute to solving the problem. As the example illustrates, planning and appropriate human resource policies can alleviate some of the effects of ageing.

The departure of ageing public servants contributes to the challenge of securing continuity in the public sector in terms of *esprit de corps*, institutional memory and networks. Yet, calling to mind that not only excellence but also mediocrity is emulated by staff, the reconfiguration of an ageing public service may prove a blessing in disguise for countries where the public sector has suffered from entrenched and non-cooperative silos of staff as well as lacklustre performance.

Departure of senior officials threatens continuity

Shortage of skilled labour

Another potential consequence of an ageing population and declining fertility rates is a decrease in the domestic supply of labour and hence a tighter labour market, which is further exacerbated by the so-called "brain drain" (see also section on "Labour migration"). This augments the difficulty of attracting enough high-quality recruits to the public service eventually contributing to the running down of the public sector. There are at least two possible solutions to this problem. One is to pay much closer attention than has recently been the case in many countries to raising the attractiveness of the civil service as a career, including more detailed attention to individual career planning through retention or promotion strategies, as is the case of China.

The pool of talent is shrinking in some countries

In China, the challenge is being faced by devoting greater effort to strategic and long-term human resource planning as well as through more rigorous workload analysis in an attempt to allocate scarce talent more rationally. Efforts are being made to raise the prestige and overall professionalism of the public service in order to increase the attractiveness of a public service career. More effort is being put into training and retraining (for example, a new nation-wide Master of Public Administration). Deliberate efforts are also being made to identify and groom talented individuals through special assignments and job rotation. All of this requires concerted effort and coordination of the kind that only well-supported, adequately resourced human resource departments can muster.

A second solution to potential or growing skills shortages, applicable mainly to richer countries, is to import public sector labour with the required skills through migration. This is part of a wider process by which the developed economies fill gaps in their labour forces as the domestic labour supply declines. Where the demand for labour from developed economies creates a significant level of outward migration of skilled workers, this situation is referred to as "brain drain". This issue is considered in the next section.

The growing global search for skilled labour by developed countries with ageing populations also contributes to the phenomenon of outsourcing, whereby corporations in economies such as the United States shift some of their activities to locations across the world where the right kind of labour is available at a lower price. This adds to the fierce competition for the supply of well-educated, skilled workers in poorer countries and contributes to the existing pressures on their civil services to attract high-quality recruits.

In sum, an ageing population, which usually is reflected in the ageing of the civil service, is a multidimensional problem with differential impact according to circumstances. Pension reform is a vital issue for most countries and with profound consequences for human resource policies and practices. If benefits of public sector workers are significantly reduced, the attractiveness of the civil service may decline and morale may be adversely affected. Compensatory measures to redress these effects must be adopted in these circumstances.

A rapid departure rate of senior officials because of a history of "boom and bust" in recruitment practices in the civil service makes succession planning a major strategic policy issue in government. The decline in new entrants in the workforce in some developed countries has created a replacement crisis, which has promoted accelerated labour migration from poor countries, which again has called for new strategies to stem the tide. Conventional methods—for example, increases in remuneration and improved working conditions—may need to be supplemented by more innovative solutions. Some of these issues are considered in the next chapter.

Faced with these demographic and labour-market challenges, countries are developing new human resource strategies and policies. Fundamental issues of staff recruitment, development and succession are being confronted anew. In the process, important principles of strategic human resource planning are being reaffirmed and lessons are being learned where they had been forgotten or neglected. These issues are addressed in greater detail later in the present report.

Labour migration

Labour migration of skilled people is commonly associated with the adverse effects of brain drain. The departure of a skilled migrant involves a loss of investment in previous education and training for the country of origin as well as a loss of skills and experience that could otherwise contribute to development, including future tax payments.[6] Not only does the country lose much needed talent, expertise, knowledge and skills, to the detriment of public service, but any indirect benefit to society in general is also eliminated.

Increased use of out-sourcing to developing countries increases the competition for already scarce talent

The risk of further poaching of talent is looming

Brain drain entails loss of investment in education and training as well as future income

Figure 2.

Ten developing countries with highest emigration rates of highly educated people to OECD countries, 1999–2001

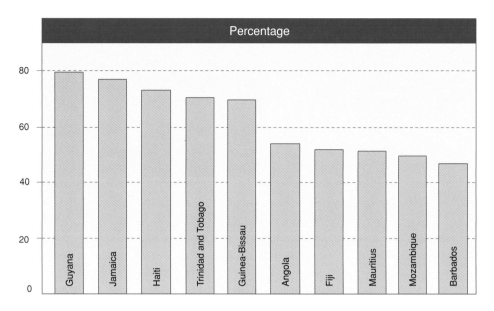

Source:
Organisation for Economic Co-operation and Development (2004).[7]

Notes:
Based on data for 113 countries. Population censuses and registers from OECD countries used (1999-2001). Population: 15+ years.

Attempts to tackle the skills gap in poor countries through education and training initiatives may have limited impact without steps to counterbalance the incentives for highly educated and skilled people to emigrate. Figure 2 shows how the emigration rates of highly educated workers from developing to OECD countries are highest in countries with small populations and in those that have emerged from civil strife in recent years, such as Angola and Mozambique. Developing and retaining a critical mass of talent is of particular importance to such countries.

Research on the scale and scope of international migration suggests a number of general conclusions about the phenomenon. First, a relatively small number of receiving developed countries account for a large proportion of the total net outflow of labour from developing countries. In 2000, the 11 major receiving developed countries accounted for 41 per cent of all international migrants.[8] Second, several such countries rely heavily on inflows from developing countries for their immigration intakes. The countries with the highest percentage of such immigrants in their total immigrant inflows are Italy (93 per cent), the United States (93 per cent) and Canada (92 per cent).[9]

Third, in most sending countries, better-educated people have higher migration rates. There are clearly both "push" and "pull" factors at play here. As to the latter, countries such as Australia, Canada, Germany and the United Kingdom have specific policies to facilitate skilled labour immigration and to limit unskilled labour and asylum seekers.[10] Fourth, although the brain drain has periodically cropped up as a policy issue in countries such as Canada, France, Germany, Sweden and the United Kingdom because the rate of return is high and because such countries receive a large number of highly skilled migrants, a better label in these cases might be "brain circulation".[11]

African and small nations have lost significant numbers of their limited talent pool owing to labour migration

A small number of countries receive the bulk of migrants

In general, better-educated people have higher migration rates

Brain drain is giving way to brain circulation in some countries

Potential benefits of labour migration

International migration, however, can also be an invaluable source of skills development and transfer, education and learning, all of which can serve to enrich both sending and host countries as migrants move back and forth. Most governments' policies to combat the effects of brain drain in developing countries increasingly address the issue through an "earn, learn and return" strategy; that is, the importance of remittances is acknowledged and migration is not discouraged, partly for this reason (indeed, it would be impractical to do so in most countries). At the same time, the loss of expertise is counterbalanced by efforts to take advantage of the enhanced skills and experience of the expatriate population, with programmes to encourage them to return, if only temporarily, or to contribute in other ways (such as investment).

Some developing countries benefit considerably from remittances (figures 3 and 4), which provide "a critical lifeline for poor families and countries alike".[12] In 2002, remittances were estimated globally at $130 billion, of which $79 billion went to developing countries. Latin America and the Caribbean and Eastern and Southern Asia were the largest recipients among developing-country regions, whereas sub-Saharan Africa received only 1.5 per cent of remittances.[13] Even though recent experiences have seen the pooling of remittances for financing local development projects in the communities of origin, a recent study has highlighted that remittances are generally spent rather than invested.[14]

One of the top recipients of remittances is the Philippines. Over 7.3 million Filipinos, or about 8 per cent of the population, live abroad. Remittances are vital to the economy, amounting in 2004 to $8.5 billion, or 10 per cent of GDP (box 6). A government agency, the Overseas Workers Welfare Administration, operates a system that facilitates safe, inexpensive remittances by overseas workers. The Government of the Philippines also offers generous incentives to encourage expatriate skilled workers to return. Its so-called "Brain Gain Network" is a database of overseas professionals and businessmen that stimulates collaboration and networking.

In some countries, specific measures have been taken to preserve the skills base of key public services, such as the health sector, and to cope with labour shortages. For example, South Africa has taken steps to combat the loss of health workers to emigration (box 7).

Figure 3.

**Ten largest developing-country
recipients of remittances, 2002**

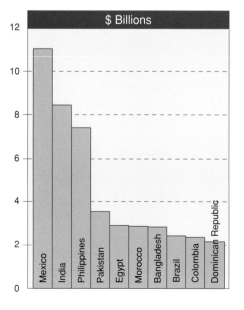

Figure 4.

**Ten developing countries with
largest ratios of remittances to
GDP, 2002**

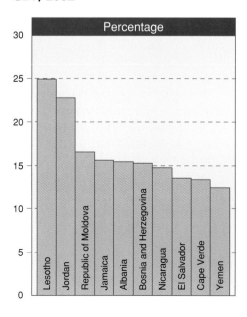

Box 6

Turning brain drain into brain gain—Philippines

When it comes to labour migration, the experience of the Philippines is undoubtedly unique. The Commission on Filipinos Overseas estimates that more than 7.3 million Filipinos, approximately 8 per cent of the country's population, currently reside abroad. In 1998, for example, nearly 15,000 teachers, engineers, nurses and computer personnel were deployed abroad through the Philippine Overseas Employment Administration (POEA). Having initially failed to prevent emigration by adopting coercive policies, the Government has instead launched a number of measures to maximize the benefits from labour migration. The results of the Philippines' experiment have been encouraging, attracting growing attention from other developing countries as a potential model in this area.

Remittances

Remittances continue to be a powerful financial force in stimulating the national economy. In 2004, the Central Bank of the Philippines reported total remittances of $8.5 billion, accounting for 10 per cent of GDP. In order to make remittances a more effective tool for national development, the Government encourages migrants to send remittances via official channels. All official workers are issued an identification card by the Overseas Workers Welfare Administration (OWWA), which is linked to dollar- or peso-denominated savings accounts in a consortium of banks. The card enables remittances to be sent both inexpensively and safely at a market-based exchange rate. The Government has also actively created a positive investment climate for Filipinos living abroad by offering tax-free investment programmes.

Return

The POEA was founded in 1995 to promote the return and reintegration of migrants. Many privileges are granted to returnees, including tax-free shopping for one year, loans for business capital at preferential rates and eligibility for subsidized scholarships. Recently, the Government decided to allow overseas workers to vote in national elections and committed a significant amount of money to overseas balloting. It has also continued to build up networks between the migrants and the homeland, and psychological counselling services are being offered through a network of offices abroad to strengthen the maintenance of "Filipino values". In addition, the Government has created the Philippines Brain Gain Network (BGN). Since 1992, the BGN has created a large human resource database of experts, potential investors and partners overseas for business networking, joint collaboration and foreign investments.

Regulation

The Government retains a regulatory role to protect workers from abuse and illegal recruitment. In order to work abroad, Filipinos must be recruited either by a licensed recruiter or a Government agency, or have their contract approved by the POEA and enrol in the official benefits programme. To encourage official labour migration, the Government offers migrants a number of benefits, including pre-migration training in social and working conditions abroad, life insurance and pension plans, medical insurance and tuition assistance for the migrants and their families, and eligibility for pre-departure and emergency loans. Registration for these benefits, which is administered by the OWWA, is compulsory and costs less than $200 per year. This service will be self-funded and paid for by the recruitment agency, presumably out of the worker's wages, or directly by the migrant if the latter has an independent contract.

Sources:
See Bibliography.

Box 7

Stemming the brain drain—South Africa

Destination-country statistics show that in 2001, more than 23,400 South African health professionals, or approximately 10 per cent of all registered practitioners in this field, were working in Australia, Canada, New Zealand, the United Kingdom and the United States. The brain drain in the public health sector in South Africa derives from a combination of push-and-pull factors.

Push factors include low salaries and benefits, unsafe working conditions, degraded health care infrastructure and inadequate opportunities for career development. Pull factors include the high transferability of medical qualifications, active foreign recruitment, higher remuneration and the shortages of health professionals in destination countries. The brain drain has undermined the Government's efforts to improve the quality of public health, especially at a time when the HIV/AIDS epidemic is seriously increasing the demands on the health system. It has also wasted substantial public training budgets. To address this growing problem, the Government of South Africa recently introduced a series of measures to retain professionals and to encourage the immigration of foreigners as well as the return of nationals working abroad.

Introduction of compulsory community service

Introduced in 1999, compulsory community service requires qualified doctors to serve at least one year in a disadvantaged part of the country after completing medical training. In 2007, this scheme is expected to be introduced to other categories of health professionals, such as nurses. The results achieved to date have been encouraging. By the end of 2003, 92 per cent of graduating doctors stayed in the country, and most of them served in the country's rural areas.

Improvements in conditions of service

The Government recently signalled its intention to improve pay and working conditions in the public health sector. In January 2003, the Treasury accepted the request of the Department of Health to increase allowances paid to physicians in priority rural areas. Average pay, including benefits, was increased by almost 5 per cent for generalists, over 12 per cent for specialists and 14 per cent for professional nurses. Non-financial incentives, such as housing and social benefits, were also introduced.

Cooperation with destination countries

The Government has negotiated bilateral and multilateral agreements with its major destination countries in order to curb the emigration of health professionals. The National Health Service (NHS) of the United Kingdom has developed a code of practice for international recruitment under which the British authorities agree not to organize recruiting campaigns for health professionals in South Africa and 153 other countries. Progress has also been made within the Commonwealth towards the definition of minimum ethical criteria for recruitment in the public health sector.

Building networks

Initiated in 1998, the South African Network of Skills Abroad (SANSA) aims to convert brain drain into brain gain by matching local shortages of skills with national expertise residing overseas. Towards this goal, SANSA has established an extensive human resource database to facilitate knowledge-sharing and networking.

Recruiting foreign health professionals

Acknowledging South Africa's need for skilled immigrants, the Government enacted a new law in March 2003 to encourage immigration of foreign professionals and to improve control of the entry of

Box 7 (cont'd)

undesirable migrants. Furthermore, South Africa has also reached agreements with several countries whose physicians could practise in the country for a predefined period with approvals from their national authorities. The best known is the programme for Cuban doctors, initiated in 1996. In 2003, there were 450 Cuban physicians practising in South Africa, most of them working in remote rural communities. This number accounted for approximately 20 per cent of emigrated physicians during the same period.

Sources:
See Bibliography.

It has been estimated that more than 23,000 South African registered health professionals (or 10 per cent of the total) are working overseas in countries such as Australia, Canada, the United Kingdom and the United States. A coordinated programme is in place to try to stem the tide. It comprises improvements in local wages and conditions; new regulations that require locally trained health-sector graduates to serve for a period in areas of special need in South Africa; and cooperation with destination countries. It also includes international databases to try to track and keep in touch with overseas South African experts (similar to the brain-gain strategy of the Government of the Philippines) and recruitment in other labour markets to try to attract professionals to come to South Africa. This last strategy highlights the potential danger of a vicious cycle of "beggar thy neighbour". Within the Commonwealth, the problem has been acknowledged by member Governments and steps have been taken to obtain agreement on a set of principles for ethical practices in recruiting overseas skills in the public health sector.

So far, this section has examined labour migration as a broad phenomenon. The global integration of labour markets is still modest. While there has been an increase in bilateral and global agreements on trade in goods, the liberalization of services and labour markets has proceeded much more slowly. Thus, the temporary movement of labour is still small relative to the size of labour markets in most countries. The temporary movement of natural persons (TMNP) represents one of four modes of service delivery recognized by the World Trade Organization's General Agreement on Trade in Services (GATS). It refers to the entry and temporary stay of persons for the purpose of providing a service (e.g., accountants, doctors or teachers).

The global integration of labour markets is still modest

The liberalization of labour markets for highly skilled labour is of particular importance to countries endowed with a significant mass of talent, such as China and India. For smaller countries, liberalization may exacerbate an already perilous exodus of skilled labour. Generating clear incentives for workers to return is important.[16] One measure could be withholding a portion of earnings until migrants return home. Such a forced savings scheme could also act to induce investment in the home country. Another approach could be the reduction of quotas for countries with low ratios of returnees. Although this has the potential of punishing the worst-off countries, sending countries could be motivated to actively attract temporary movers.

Generating incentives for migrants to return is critical

Some recent developments are likely to mitigate the adverse effects of labour migration. For example, the explosion of Internet connections has contributed to the "death of distance", thus opening up new doors for reduction of the impact of the brain drain by allowing expatriate nationals to stay in closer touch with their native countries and even to contribute directly to economic development. The Africa Union's policy of considering Africans in the diaspora as the fifth region of the continent is one initiative in this regard. Other interesting initiatives in this area include the Transfer of Knowledge through Expatriate Nationals (TOKTEN) programme, initiated by UNDP and presently managed by the United

Nations Volunteers, and the Digital Diaspora Network, launched by the United Nations Information and Communication Technologies (ICT) Task Force to promote development through the use of ICTs.

HIV/AIDS

HIV/AIDS is the leading cause of death in sub-Saharan Africa

HIV/AIDS has become the fourth most common cause of death in the world and it is the leading cause of death in sub-Saharan Africa. The severity of the epidemic is illustrated in figures 5 and 6.

HIV/AIDS disrupts the supply of prospective employees . . .

The increasing incidence of HIV/AIDS, especially in developing countries, is a significant challenge facing public administrations as employers. Given that the disease normally affects younger adults and those in the most economically productive phases of their lives, HIV/AIDS has the potential to reduce the pool of prospective employees and shrink the economic productivity of many countries. It has been estimated that in the eight African countries with the highest prevalence rates, the male and female working populations in 2020 will be smaller by just under 20 per cent than they would have been in the absence of AIDS.[17] In Malawi, it is estimated that about 25 per cent of the urban workforce will die by 2009 as a result of the rapid spread of HIV/AIDS (box 8). The demographic profile in such countries will change, with a dramatic rise in the proportion of young people in the population.

The impact on the labour market goes further:

. . . and has staggering consequences for government performance

- A loss of significant numbers of skilled workers, including in the public sector (there is a tendency for more highly skilled, professional groups to suffer higher levels of HIV/AIDS-related deaths);

Figure 5.

Ten developing countries with highest proportion of adults living with HIV, 2003

Source:
Joint United Nations Programme on HIV/AIDS (2004).[18]

Notes: Estimates. Adult signifies person aged 15 to 49 years.

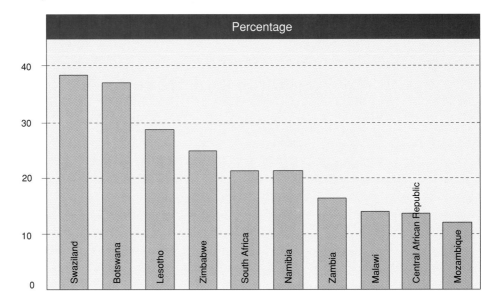

Figure 6.
Ten developing countries with the most adults living with HIV, 2003

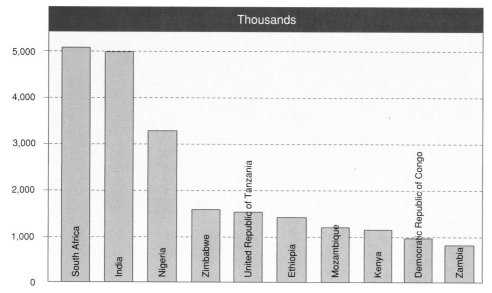

Source:
Joint United Nations
Programme on HIV/AIDS
(2004).[18]

Notes: Estimates. Adult
signifies person aged 15
to 49 years.

- High levels of absenteeism and leave without pay by those suffering from the condition (especially in the public sector, where leave provisions tend to be more generous); and

- Increasing levels of families headed by children, child poverty and lack of preparedness for skilled work for new entrants to the workforce, particularly with the growing numbers of orphans.

Furthermore, there is a spillover impact on the public sector, such as increased demands for public services and social assistance and a loss of revenue (estimated, in the case of Botswana, to be 20 per cent over the next twenty years).[19]

Box 8

The impact of HIV/AIDS on the public service—Malawi

It is estimated that in Malawi, about 25 per cent of the urban workforce will die by 2009 as the result of the rapid spread of HIV/AIDS. With a prevalence rate among adults (ages 15–49) of approximately 15 per cent—almost twice the rate of other countries in sub-Saharan Africa—the HIV/AIDS epidemic has already inflicted a heavy burden on both the current and the future workforce in the Malawi public service.

Not only is the capacity of the Government to provide health-related services to those affected stretched to its limit, but organizations also have to deal with the serious impact of this pandemic on the human resources in the public service. For example, between 1990 and 2000, the largest and most influential ministries in Malawi suffered from an increasing number of deaths of civil servants. In the late 1990s, the actual mortality rate was more than six times higher than the rate prior to the discovery of the first AIDS case, with young adults accounting for the majority of the increase (see figure).

Box 8 (cont'd)

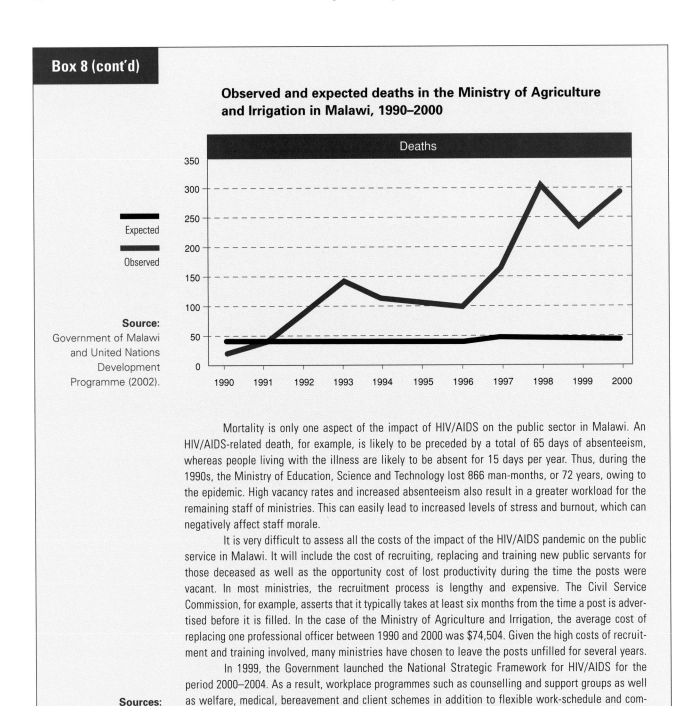

Observed and expected deaths in the Ministry of Agriculture and Irrigation in Malawi, 1990–2000

Expected

Observed

Source:
Government of Malawi and United Nations Development Programme (2002).

Mortality is only one aspect of the impact of HIV/AIDS on the public sector in Malawi. An HIV/AIDS-related death, for example, is likely to be preceded by a total of 65 days of absenteeism, whereas people living with the illness are likely to be absent for 15 days per year. Thus, during the 1990s, the Ministry of Education, Science and Technology lost 866 man-months, or 72 years, owing to the epidemic. High vacancy rates and increased absenteeism also result in a greater workload for the remaining staff of ministries. This can easily lead to increased levels of stress and burnout, which can negatively affect staff morale.

It is very difficult to assess all the costs of the impact of the HIV/AIDS pandemic on the public service in Malawi. It will include the cost of recruiting, replacing and training new public servants for those deceased as well as the opportunity cost of lost productivity during the time the posts were vacant. In most ministries, the recruitment process is lengthy and expensive. The Civil Service Commission, for example, asserts that it typically takes at least six months from the time a post is advertised before it is filled. In the case of the Ministry of Agriculture and Irrigation, the average cost of replacing one professional officer between 1990 and 2000 was $74,504. Given the high costs of recruitment and training involved, many ministries have chosen to leave the posts unfilled for several years.

In 1999, the Government launched the National Strategic Framework for HIV/AIDS for the period 2000–2004. As a result, workplace programmes such as counselling and support groups as well

Sources:
See Bibliography.

as welfare, medical, bereavement and client schemes in addition to flexible work-schedule and compassionate leave policies for infected persons have been put in place.

The management of HIV/AIDS issues in the work place presents many dilemmas. Mortality is only one aspect of the problem to be managed. In Malawi, HIV/AIDS-related death is on average preceded by 65 days of absenteeism (compared with an annual norm of 15 days). This, in addition to the stress caused by the loss of colleagues, places strain on other workers, causing burnout and loss of efficiency as well as a higher attrition rate.

Managing in an HIV/AIDS environment

Employees with HIV/AIDS present specific challenges in terms of personnel and management practices. Workers with HIV/AIDS are likely to experience some degree of limitation in terms of their performance as well as social isolation and psychological problems, especially if faced with disclosure. Policy questions arise about the role of compulsory screening and/or the value of requiring candidates to declare their condition at the point of application or appointment. Early counselling support may be invaluable for those tested. There is a need for adjustment for all concerned, not just those with the illness. How to deal with these problems is clearly a whole-of-government responsibility, going far beyond HRM responsibilities. At the same time, there is a clear set of challenges and impacts, and a need for responses, within the human resource domain.

There is still widespread misunderstanding about HIV/AIDS to the extent that it could affect the performance of both the employees with the condition and their colleagues. The need is clear for policies on the employment of people with HIV/AIDS, including their rights and obligations, unambiguous guidelines for employees in terms of working with people with the condition, and specific support for those having to manage teams that include someone with the illness. Measures to combat discrimination are necessary, including not only statutory provisions—as, for instance, the 2001 amendment to the South African Public Service Regulations—but also codes of practice and training to raise awareness.

There is a clear need for policies on employment of people with HIV/AIDS . . .

Many governments and public organizations have taken steps to deal with the management of HIV/AIDS in the work place. For example, the Department of Public Service and Administration (DPSA) in South Africa has adopted a comprehensive policy that includes strategies for prevention; voluntary counselling and testing (VCT) and support for those infected and affected; education; resources and leadership to implement work-place programmes on HIV/AIDS and sexually transmitted diseases; creation of a non-discriminatory environment; and protection of confidentiality of those who voluntarily disclose their HIV status. Minimum standards and a manual of best practices have been promulgated; education and awareness programmes have been mandated; and HIV/AIDS committees have been set up in each department.

The DPSA has acknowledged a number of concerns over implementation of this strategy:

- Lack of integration of HIV/AIDS policies and programmes into broader wellness initiatives and human resource practices;
- A tendency to allocate HIV/AIDS responsibilities to junior officials with limited skills, experience and influence;
- Limited data on HIV prevalence rates and the impact of HIV/AIDS on the work place; and
- Inadequate understanding of specific work-place challenges such as the existence of stereotypes and prejudices.

Reports on progress in implementation suggest that one of the most serious problems is the unwillingness of employees to participate in the VCT schemes, partly for fear of discrimination. A further serious problem is the lack of health insurance for the majority of public service workers. The Government of South Africa has announced its intention to introduce a new medical scheme in order to increase its coverage and make it more affordable.[20]

. . . and such policies must be supported from the centre of government

In summary, all public organizations need a clear employment policy on HIV/ AIDS in the work place. Such a policy must be supported from the centre of government hierarchy and be understood and pursued in all government agencies; it should be comprehensive, well publicized and well understood by all employees, not simply personnel/human resource specialists. Organizations need to have a clearly articulated position on issues such as testing, disclosure, absenteeism (including sick pay) and support services. Managers may need specific support and advice in dealing with employees with this condition.

Notes

1   United Nations (2003). World Population Prospects: The 2002 Revision. Supplementary Tabulations. (POP/DB/WPP/Rev.2002/1). CD-Rom.

2   Gujral., I.K. (2001). Global Ageing and the Role of South Asia. Keynote Address at the 2nd Plenary of the Commission on Global Ageing. Available from http://www.csis.org/gai/ Zurich/speeches/gujral.html

3   United Nations (2003). World Population Prospects: The 2002 Revision. Department of Economic and Social Affairs. Sales No. E.03.XIII.8.

4   Organisation for Economic Co-operation and Development (2002). Highlights of Public Sector Pay and Employment Trends: 2002 Update. Public Management Committee. Paris: OECD. Available from http://www.olis.oecd.org/olis/2002doc.nsf/LinkTo/PUMA-HRM(2002)7

5   Podger, Andrew S. (2004). Innovation with integrity—the public sector leadership imperative to 2020. Australian Journal of Public Administration, vol. 63, issue 1 (March), pp. 14–15.

6   United Nations (2004). World Economic and Social Survey 2004: International Migration. Department of Economic and Social Affairs. Sales No. E.04.II.C.3. Available from http://www.un.org/esa/policy/wess/

7   Organisation for Economic Co-operation and Development (2004). Database on immigrants and expatriates. Available from http://www.oecd.org/dataoecd/31/16/34107878.xls, based on the following sources: Daniel Cohen and Marcelo Soto (2001). Growth and Human Capital: Good Data, Good Results. Technical Papers No. 179. OECD Development Centre. Available from http://www.oecd.org/dataoecd/ 33/12/2669509.pdf; and Robert J. Barro and Jong-Wha Lee (2000). International Data on Educational Attainment: Updates and Implications. Working Paper 7911. National Bureau of Economic Research. Available from http://www.nber.org/papers/w7911

8   United Nations (2004). Op. cit., pp. 30–31.

9   Grieco, Elizabeth and Kimberly A. Hamilton (2004). Realizing the potential of migrant "earn, learn, and return" strategies: does policy matter? Washington, D.C.: Migration Policy Institute. Available from http://www.cgdev.org/rankingtherich/docs/Migration_2004.pdf

10   Ibid., p. 20.

11   Organisation for Economic Co-operation and Development (2002). International Mobility of the Highly Skilled. Policy Brief (July). Available from http://www.oecd.org/dataoecd/9/20/1950028.pdf

12   Grieco and Hamilton (2004). Op. cit., p. 2.

13   United Nations (2004). Op. cit.: see "Remittances", pp. 102–111.

14   Chami, Ralph, Connel Fullenkamp and Jahjah Samir (2003). Are Immigrant Remittance Flows a Source of Capital for Development? IMF Working Paper 189. Available from http://www.imf.org/external/pubs/ft/wp/2003/wp03189.pdf

15   United Nations (2004). Op. cit.

16   Birdsall, Nancy, Dani Rodrik and Arvind Subramanian (2005). How to help poor countries. Foreign Affairs, vol. 84, no. 4. July/August.

17   The eight countries were: Botswana, Kenya, Malawi, Mozambique, Namibia, Rwanda, South Africa and Zimbabwe.

18   Joint United Nations Programme on HIV/AIDS (2004). *2004 Report on the Global AIDS Epidemic: 4th Global Report*. Geneva: UNAIDS. Available from http://www.unaids.org/bangkok2004/GAR2004_html/GAR2004_00_en.htm

19   Joint United Nations Programme on HIV/AIDS (2004). Op. cit.

20   Public Service and Administration Portfolio Committee (2002). Impact of HIV/AIDS on Public Servants: Briefing. Parliamentary Monitoring Group, South Africa. 25 September. Available from http://www.pmg.org.za/viewminute.php?id=2097; and (2004). Management of HIV/AIDS in Public Service: Briefing. 20 October. Available from http://www.pmg.org.za/viewminute.php?id=4718

Chapter IV
The mixed results of HRM reform

In responding and adapting to the socio-economic challenges discussed in the previous chapter as well as other important concerns, public administration systems around the world have had to improvise and innovate. The examples in the previous sections illustrate that governments have been forced to reassess critical factors underlying human resource strategies and practices, refocusing on issues of recruitment and retention of scarce talent and valuable experience, dealing with questions of morale and individual staff welfare and development needs, and bringing these matters closer to the centre of governments' strategic planning processes.

Governments have also had to face up to changing perceptions of needs and priorities in public administration theory and practice, with direct implications for HRM. These reform challenges have many sources: public disenchantment with government and public service performance; growing fiscal and policy pressures due to rising expectations; academic theory and fashion; diffusion of "best practices"; major policy shifts both within countries and internationally caused by changes of government, changes of regime and wider global developments such as economic or financial crises or demographic shifts; and (in the case of e-government) technological change.

With the benefit of hindsight, it can be observed that some facets of reform have actually damaged some of the core capacities necessary for developing sound human resource practices; others have improved or restored these capacities. In this chapter, we will examine some of the lessons learned from important reform initiatives during the 1980s and 1990s: structural adjustment and downsizing; managerial reforms under the banner of NPM; labour relations; and diversity management.

Some facets of reform have damaged core capacities necessary for developing sound HRM practices

Structural adjustment and downsizing

One way of assessing the importance of different HRM policy initiatives is to look at the scale of their adoption. Between 1987 and 1996, for example, the World Bank assisted no fewer than 68 developing countries and transition economies with staffing reform programmes.[1] China, the world's most populous nation, embarked in 1998 on a reform programme designed to cut the number of its civil servants by half—in other words, by a projected four million people[2]—and similarly dramatic reports are also available from countries such as Bolivia and Uganda.

Even in industrialized countries, the scale of staff reductions has been spectacular: downsizing programmes were carried out between 1987 and 1992 in the public sectors of 22 of the 27 member countries of OECD, making it by some distance the most widespread human resource initiative during that period.[3] The Australian Public Service, for example, was reduced from 181,000 to 143,000 staff between 1986 and 1996, and in Finland, the number of state employees funded from the central budget fell by almost 40 per cent between 1989 and 1995.

Structural adjustment measures in developing countries often resulted in a set of harsh measures that lacked support and legitimacy because of their social impact, to the detriment of other reforms that might have resulted in improvements in administrative capacities. Indeed, it has been argued that the emphasis on downsizing and related structural adjustment

HRM reforms has previously been heavily focused on staff reductions

Structural adjustments lacked both support and legitimacy

measures may have given reform a bad name: reform across a wider spectrum was "stigmatized by the pains of such first-wave structural reform".[4] Moreover, only modest results were achieved in the downsizing programmes that were supported by loans and other external assistance.

Many of the measures adopted were shallow or did not last. Although several African countries conducted ministry-by-ministry audits of civil service functions, only in a few cases were these followed up with high-impact initiatives such as merging or dissolving a significant number of ministries.[5] Much of the initial reduction in the number of employees was achieved through tackling "ghost" and temporary workers and then by the introduction of early retirement and voluntary retrenchment programmes with generous severance deals. Retrenched workers returned through "revolving doors"; demands for essential services required new hiring; and the great bulk of those retrenched were on such low wages that savings were small.[6] Real public employment did fall for a while but then bottomed out, with political pressures prompting subsequent rises in some cases.

In many ways, downsizing programmes reflected an inherent weakness in HRM systems, which could not strike a balance between the tasks at hand and the human resource requirements, or the "ins" or "outs" of the public service. Therefore, reducing the number of staff without redefining the mission and functions of the government did not address the underlying problem.

On the whole, significant improvements did not result from such efforts. As one assessment put it, "fiscally driven reductions of state employment and functions have gone too far and have not led to general and significant efficiency and accountability improvements".[7] Insufficient attention was paid to the political dynamics of various reform interventions—in particular, coping with adverse reactions to the reforms themselves. This aspect was highlighted in the Benin case discussed in chapter II.

The public service in many of the countries subject to these measures was traditionally seen as a provider of secure employment. Reductions in salaries were often skewed towards the better paid in order not to cause resentment among the large voting population of lower-paid workers. However, the erosion of public sector salaries at the higher levels compared with those in the private sector can be demotivating to the extent that skilled professionals are tempted to leave for better-paid non-government jobs. This is a tough scenario to manage. Retaining skilled employees, maintaining their motivation and finding measures for enhancing their performance and curbing the public sector wage bill require a fine balancing act. In fact, in many places, there is an urgent need to increase remuneration for managerial positions, which is further dealt with in chapter V.

This climate of "defeatism" in the public sector, however, needs to give way to a climate of more active human resource management, where public agencies and their managers are working with the staff to help them to contribute to achieving the agencies' strategic objectives and to develop themselves. At the outset, it must be stated that the governments that devoted so much energy to curtailing spending on staff were partly right: staff are a cost. Spending on salaries, pensions and allowances consumes the lion's share of public expenditure in most developing countries. With ministries of finance in the lead throughout the 1980s and 1990s as governments went to great lengths to rein in public expenditure (figure 7), policy-makers could be forgiven for viewing staff exclusively in terms of costs that needed to be slashed. Many governments did need to act to contain spending and some undoubtedly still do.

Perhaps there is also a more profound reason why governments have treated staff as a cost: the ingrained "defeatism" among managers in the public sector that led them to think of employees as a force of nature that could neither be managed nor developed. In governments where central staffing control was strong, line managers had little practical control

Figure 7.

Central government expenditure on wages in 49 developing countries, 1980–1999

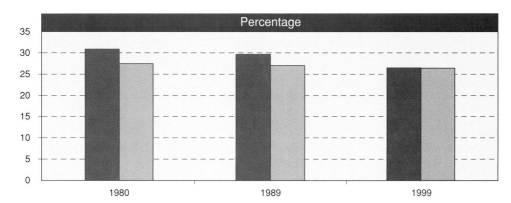

Gov't expenditure
as per cent of GDP

Wages as per cent
of gov't expenditure

Source:
UN/DESA based on World
Bank, *World Development
Indicators*.

Notes:
Five year averages
centred on 1980, 1989
and 1999. Averages of
1980 and 1999 used as
1989 data for Senegal,
Sudan and Uganda.

over the staff whom, in theory, they supervised. For example, a manager might wake up one day discovering that a staff member had been transferred, literally overnight, into or out of the department in response to what the manager might well consider as the inscrutable whim of the central staffing office. In such an HRM environment, managers are bound to feel that there is little point in trying to influence the way that staff perform their work.

Therefore, in the latter half of the 1990s, many governments gradually began to move away from downsizing to more focused management of the human resources in the public sector, as mentioned earlier. Regular reporting by OECD on issues relating to staff management in the public sector is one example of such growing emphasis on HRM in the industrialized world. Gradually, several governments in developing countries also realized the limitations of downsizing programmes, which often did not achieve meaningful staff reductions, as stated before. In addition, downsizing programmes did not contribute much to enhancing efficiency and effectiveness in the public sector.

> The focused management of human resources has emerged as a viable approach . . .

By the advent of the twenty-first century, downsizing initiatives in OECD countries had become significantly less prominent, presumably indicating that the battle had been won, in some countries at least. Other HRM measures reported in the 1994 survey were still important—notably devolution of management authority to line ministries and agencies and the introduction of performance management and appraisal, sometimes including a performance-related pay element—though now joined by new measures. These included improving the gender and ethnic diversity of the workforce and greater use of staff attitude surveys and staff forums as well as the need to develop an overall framework for staff management.

> . . . including diversity issues and participatory activities

New public management: *lessons learned*

As described in chapter I, NPM has been promoted as a "global model", often recommended by influential international agencies. When these agencies bring assistance and advice to developing countries, the temptation is merely to copy when, in fact, the challenge is to adapt and select. With this in mind, the present section examines some lessons from several decades of NPM diffusion and adoption by many governments, both in the general area of public sector reform and more specifically in the area of HRM. In brief, while the lessons of NPM in countries where it originated are ambiguous, the experience of NPM in developing countries is even more starkly so.

> Lessons of NPM are ambiguous

> The temptation is merely to copy when, in fact, the challenge is to adapt and select

NPM was essentially doctrine-driven, especially in its early years. A common phenomenon among the reform-minded progenitors of NPM was their rush to implement and extend their initiatives before evaluating the consequences. However, even if rigorous evaluations have been few and far between, the lessons of experience have pointed to some common trends in HRM due to the spread of NPM doctrine and practices:

- HRM in the public sector became similar to its private sector counterparts. Economic efficiency was one of the most important standards of reform, achieved, for instance, by reducing the size of the public sector;

- Many efforts were made to give line ministries and/or line managers greater flexibility and freedom in HRM through various decentralization and devolution policies; and

- In return for providing greater flexibility and freedom to agencies, governments tried to secure accountability of line ministries and/or line managers in HRM by stressing the performance and ethics of the civil service.[8]

There are only a handful of governance systems that are systematically structured to reflect NPM doctrine and to make full use of the NPM tool-kit. Perhaps the Anglo-Saxon countries of Australia, New Zealand and the United Kingdom are the best-known examples. The experience of Australia, for example, shows that devolved management coupled with a set of clear central goals and policies (for example, cost-cutting) can be an effective instrument for achieving change. From the mid-1980s, NPM-style reforms were driven largely by transforming the public-expenditure management process under the guidance of the Department of Finance. Managerial reforms, such as one-line budgets and performance monitoring of programme outputs and outcomes, were accompanied by, among other things, the creation of internal markets, semi-autonomous agencies, user fees and charges set to recover costs and contracting-out.

Throughout these years, the Government of Australia acquired the reputation of being a sound financial manager, meeting budget targets, showing fiscal discipline and successfully targeting and cutting expenditures where needs and circumstances required. Much of this was achieved by more targeted strategic management at the agency level, bringing efficiency gains. At the same time, it required strong political direction and some old-fashioned fiscal discipline and controls to "squeeze" these savings from the system.

Outsourcing: *a double-edged sword*

Achievements in improving efficiency (i.e., technical or productive efficiency) are the most commonly claimed benefits of NPM initiatives. The claim is that new market-like constraints and incentives push managers to improve efficiency. For example, contracting-out or outsourcing is said to bring efficiency gains (narrowly defined). It may also bring improvements in service quality, as properly managed contracting requires a systematic approach to monitoring and quality assurance, which focuses increased attention on service delivery. Outsourcing also takes advantage of skills and technology available in the private sector and is commonly adopted to provide back-office information technology services. The United Kingdom has been a leader in contracting out what were formerly in-house functions and services, for example in the National Health Service (NHS) (box 9). There, a recent development has been the growth of public-private partnerships (PPPs) for the provision of key support services.

Box 9

Outsourcing public services:
the National Health Service—United Kingdom

Globally, the United Kingdom has been a leader in the application of outsourcing in the public sector. Initially, the use of outsourcing was limited mainly to administrative and information technology (IT)-related "back-office" functions, but more recently, it has been expanded into other "front-line" services as well. This includes catering and the delivery of health services.

In 2003, for example, a privately run hospital in Surrey became a diagnosis and treatment centre (DTC), providing routine surgery, testing and outpatient services exclusively for the National Health Service (NHS). The staff of independent-sector DTCs are private sector employees. Both United Kingdom and overseas health care companies have since been invited to bid for the operation of additional DTCs. The private sector is also being offered the possibility of operating chains of DTCs for different types of medical treatments.

Even though outsourcing plays an increasing role in the delivery of front-line health services in the United Kingdom, it still remains heavily focused on back-office functions. A major contributor to the recent large increase in the application of outsourcing in the health sector has been the National Programme for Information Technology (NPfIT). The value of IT contracts rose almost seven-fold from £1billion in 2002/2003 to around £6.9billion by the end of 2003/2004. The NPfIT, inter alia, has initiated the establishment of a number of electronic systems, such as to manage the records of patients as well as the appointment and registration processes.

As part of health sector reform, the NHS Shared Financial Services, which currently provides back-office functions, such as accounting, budgets, value-added tax (VAT) and supplier invoice settlement for a number of NHS organizations, announced in November 2004 that it would transform itself into a joint venture partnership with a private company. The ownership of the new firm, called NHS Shared Business Services Limited, will be divided evenly between the Government and its private-sector partner. Staff will be transferred to the private company but will retain NHS conditions of service as per the 1981 Transfer of Undertakings (Protection of Employment) Regulations.

While the proponents of outsourcing believe that it can generate significant efficiency gains and cost savings, others are more skeptical. The NPfIT, for example, has come under criticism for being too ambitious as well as for significant budget overruns and lack of proper evaluation of the costs and benefits of the outsourcing option. In addition, UNISON, Britain's biggest trade union, and other critics from the health professions have expressed fears that the DTCs will charge higher fees than those currently applied in the public health system and poach NHS staff, thereby further draining its limited human resources, partly because the DTCs have been allowed to employ seconded NHS staff.

Sources:
See Bibliography.

Outsourcing, however, should be undertaken only with great care. A recent experience in the municipality of Copenhagen in Denmark illustrates this point. In 2003, the municipality outsourced payroll management of 50,000 employees to a private consulting company. It was envisaged that this arrangement would generate cost savings for the municipality of around $7 million over a period of six years. Yet the outsourcing is now expected to increase costs by $6 million in 2005 alone. Thousands of employees received inaccurate pay checks in 2004, leading the Labour Court to rule in early 2005 that the collective agreement between the employer and employees had been violated by the municipality because of the lack of timely and correct salary payments. Subsequently, the consulting company agreed to pay $2.5 million in compensation to the municipality.[9]

Some governments have begun to use outsourcing in the security and military sectors through private military firms and private military contractors. This practice, however, has

... it should be undertaken with great care

Outsourcing in the
security and military
sector is emerging as
a significant trend

been fraught with controversy, as no country has yet developed clear policies regarding the regulation of such firms. For example, the recruitment, screening and hiring of individuals for public military roles are, by definition, left in private hands, which raises some important accountability, oversight and performance issues. It has also been pointed out that the profit motive of contractors may not always be congruent with the interests of the respective governments.

Caution is also needed in case successes associated with outsourcing are attributed to the wrong causes. So-called efficiency gains in labour-intensive functions and services are generally a result of contracting-out, under which private sector workers have less favourable pay and working conditions than their public sector counterparts. The savings are primarily a spillover effect of marketization rather than the direct result of a new set of constraints or incentives for managers. In such cases, outsourcing reflects a choice, depressing wages and conditions for publicly funded workers providing public services.

Deregulation of HRM:
creating new bureaucratic control

Deregulation of HRM
is often accompanied
by new emphasis
on re-regulation

Paradoxically, deregulation to "let managers manage" is typically accompanied by re-regulation that imposes new, and perhaps more burdensome, constraints. Sometimes, these are in the style of market-type mechanisms aimed at improving coordination or reliance on "self-regulation" within new frameworks of accountability and transparency (such as performance indicators). However, these often appear to be no less intrusive or bothersome to managers than old-style by-the-book controls and inspections.

Trends in New Zealand, the United Kingdom and elsewhere demonstrate a large and growing apparatus of regulation erected over and above the leaner, devolved systems of management, staffing and service delivery as a result of NPM reforms.[10] Inspection and audit mechanisms to implement the new NPM-style "arms-length" monitoring have grown disproportionately. What is saved on the one hand may be eaten up by new overheads on the other.

This also illustrates another aspect of what has been learned from the experience of NPM. For example, what may have appeared to be logical, simple solutions to well-defined problems may turn out to be only half the story. Most administrative problems are of the "on the one hand . . . on the other" kind: they are messy and full of conflicting requirements. Autonomy and devolved management are good ideas for focusing single-mindedly on an important objective but bad ideas when it is important to coordinate with some other equally important objective. This is a typical administrative dilemma. Like the swings of a pendulum, governments shift from one pole to another in the search for the "ideal point". Indeed, governments in countries where NPM got an early start have been seen to react against some of its supposed successes, instituting "joined-up government" to restore coordination or putting in place new instruments of policy control.

Performance-related pay:
an unwarranted panacea?

Evidence on efficiency
gains by way
of performance
pay is ambiguous

Many predicted efficiency gains of NPM are not easily observable. A good example is performance-related pay, a favourite of NPM advocates, where evidence is inconclusive and ambiguous.[11] While performance-related pay is theoretically an ideal way to reward merit in the public service, its implementation is often riddled with difficulties. Critics claim that performance pay may promote emphasis on short-term successes rather than a long-term perspective, that it involves major methodological and measurement problems, and that it can potentially demoralize "non-achievers".

The experience of some OECD countries with performance pay in the public service, for example, has not been altogether satisfactory, particularly because policy-makers often do not have an adequate understanding of the complexities involved in administering such a system. In any case, a single-minded focus on material incentives downgrades other reward and incentive measures that may be just as important, such as stability of employment and the prospect of interesting, worthwhile work. Fairness, equity and reward for loyalty and commitment to the service as a whole are built into systems of incentives and rewards in such cases.

Notwithstanding the above arguments, it is also unwise to reject performance pay entirely, as its failure may often be caused by weak design and inadequate preparation rather than inherent problems in the concept itself. An instructive illustration is the proposal

---

Box 10

Performance-related pay: *if you fail to prepare, you prepare to fail*—Mauritius

For a long time, Mauritius has had a traditional civil service pay structure with annual increments for public servants. A small link between pay and performance had been built into the system. During the 1990s, there was growing interest in Mauritius in introducing such a scheme into the public service. Instead of copying foreign models, the Ministry of Civil Service Affairs and Administrative Reforms (MCSAAR) first conducted a survey at all levels of government, local authorities and civil servants' associations in order to assess the likely receptiveness of public servants to such an innovation.

The response rate was above 55 per cent and numerous valuable comments were collected from 88 government agencies and public organizations. The figure below illustrates how well staff responded to different practices related to performance-related reward (PRR).

Performance-related reward in the Government of Mauritius

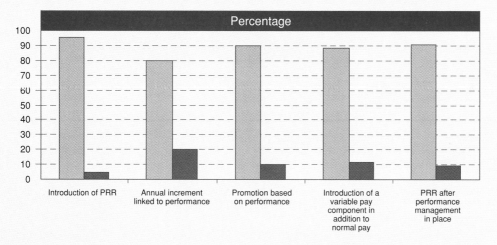

Source: Government of Mauritius (2003).

Most staff associations, including unions, expressed skepticism about the manner in which such a scheme would be introduced. The unions were also fearful that the selection process could be subject to patronage, favouritism and abuse. They therefore preferred a system rewarding organizational performance.

Box 10 (con't)

Based on the feedback, the MCSAAR concluded that, although the majority of respondents were in favour of performance-related pay, there was strong apprehension about introducing it too early as well as concern about how fairly it would be implemented. It was also felt that a performance-related pay scheme would need certain prerequisites in place, including strong support from top management, proper integration with a proper performance management and appraisal system, and an effective internal communication strategy. Given the specificity of the Mauritius environment, the reform had to be cautiously carried out in phases and on a pilot basis, with mechanisms for examining, approving, controlling and monitoring the implementation of the programme. Efficiency, diligence and commitment, for example, should be major indicators for assessing performance.

Sources:
See Bibliography.

to introduce performance-related pay in Mauritius (box 10). Staff feared that the system would encourage patronage and favouritism, and there was strong support for organizational or team-based rewards as well as individual rewards, with the caveat that transparent, objective and fair systems of appraisal of individuals must first be in place. Another example of the inherent difficulty of introducing performance-related pay is found in Germany, where Parliament rejected a proposal by the Government to introduce more flexibility into the civil service pay system.

NPM: *more than a doctrine*

Understanding NPM only as doctrine is not sufficient

The fact that an idea such as "performance" or "merit pay" can be so differently interpreted and applied in practice also warns against treating all the tools and instruments of NPM as expressions of one underlying doctrine, as discussed in chapter I; they can be adapted and used for many purposes. The transformation of NPM in local settings occurs partly because these tools, once uncoupled from the underlying doctrine, are open to multiple uses and extensions. For instance, adherence to civil service stability and continuity and to norms of mutuality and reciprocity are so strong in some political cultures that instruments stressing competition and self-management are antithetical even if the aims of improved efficiency and performance are shared. The Republic of Korea, for example, has adopted a model of public sector reform that avowedly espouses NPM principles[12] while moving in a more cautious, piecemeal manner in importing its tool-kit.

NPM tools are often adapted to local settings . . .

. . . mutating into something quite different

NPM instruments or tools applied to a local setting may even mutate into something quite different.[13] Thus, when the Government of the Hong Kong Special Administrative Region of China implemented performance-based rewards, it did so in order to encourage and reward teams of civil servants jointly responsible for a successful outcome rather than to "incentivize" individuals. This may reflect cultural norms that frown on excesses of competition in the work place (as distinct from the marketplace). A common pitfall in assessing the appropriateness of NPM for developing countries is that what appears "on the ground" as an initiative in the style of NPM is often, in fact, something very different because the underlying problems being addressed are different. Strange hybrids crop up in such cases.

NPM is sometimes perceived as solutions chasing problems, when in fact the problems require different solutions

Evaluating such reforms as a case of NPM would miss the point: they apply a surface veneer of NPM doctrine to problems other than those that such a doctrine directly addresses. In the presence of such examples of the mismatch between problems on the ground and those that NPM addresses, it could be argued that many attempts to implement NPM in developing countries may be doomed from the start. As just illustrated, many local problems in developing countries are very different from those that NPM seeks to solve. Perhaps this is a case of "solutions chasing problems" when in fact the problems require other solutions.

Leap-frogging: *a possibility?*

A different argument about the inappropriateness of NPM solutions to the problems of developing countries proposes that NPM represents a "stage of development" in public sector reform that developing countries are not yet ready to handle (see chapter II); problems addressed by earlier, traditional public administration disciplines must be dealt with first. Reliability, continuity, equity and due process need to be institutionalized, for example, ahead of responsiveness, flexibility and a "customer orientation". NPM in Western countries was feasible and appropriate only once issues such as probity, integrity, regularity and accountability had been resolved by traditional public administration.

It can be argued that this argument seems to fall into the trap of predicating all "development" on the need to follow a single path or trajectory: the trail that has been blazed by "advanced Western democracies". Such a view is open to the charge of ethnocentricity. This transfer of Western blueprints and models as if they were relevant to all times and places has aptly been labelled "institutional monocropping".[14] Crucially, such an approach is likely to miss opportunities for improvement that emerge from tapping local problem-solving capacities.[15]

Nevertheless, there is strong evidence from the experience of NPM reforms in developing countries that there are certain prerequisites for successful reform. For example, it has been argued that use of market-type mechanisms and contracting requires that a functioning formal market first be in place; that authority cannot be devolved if it is not first unified and centralized; and that accounting for outputs will not be effective as a way of monitoring unless officials are first accustomed to accounting for inputs.[16]

This point of view seems to suggest a somewhat cautious scenario in which innovation must await the slow, careful development of support systems and institutional frameworks that Western countries developed over centuries. However, the "latecomer advantage" can be a real one. So long as arguments about the need to tackle reforms in logical steps or stages are pointing to the existence of prerequisites for particular measures of improvement, a more optimistic view of possibilities is opened up. That is, "leap-frogging" may be possible, although not across the board but rather in selected priority areas: governments may not need to wait until a fully fledged, functioning traditional public administration is in place in those priority areas before implementing NPM initiatives so long as attention is paid to having in place vital accompanying administrative support systems and infrastructure relevant to each particular problem.[17]

The case of a successful local health initiative in northern Brazil, which involved both a judicious combination of tight central staffing controls (because of the pervasiveness of local patronage networks) and high levels of local operational autonomy is instructive in this regard.[18] Local autonomy afforded the health teams a sense of empowerment, which encouraged them to respond flexibly to local needs. However, this autonomy was constrained in ways that ensured that potential abuses could be avoided. The centre not only imposed tight personnel controls, but it also set performance standards, publicized them and sought feedback, deliberately encouraging local populations to monitor outcomes.

The issue here is not whether devolution can work only if it is preceded by or builds on a functioning, rule-governed bureaucracy and a well-managed system of performance measurement, but whether in deploying it, certain conditions are put in place, such as staffing procedures that ensure competence and task commitment and a set of outcome standards that facilitate transparency and accountability. In this case, the government was able to

Institutional monocropping is a potential risk

Prerequisites exist for implementing NPM for successful reform . . .

. . . and with these in place, "leap-frogging" may be possible

Planning for contingencies may facilitate "leap-frogging"

invest sufficient human and financial resources to ensure that those conditions were in place to enable "leap-frogging" to happen. However, given the general resource constraints facing governments in developing countries, the report suggests that such a strategy may not be applicable under several circumstances. In some cases, the lessons to be drawn for effective reform are about "getting the mix right" for the contingencies faced.[19]

Even with this in mind, however, circumstances sometimes require what appear to be high-risk reform strategies, that is, "getting the sequencing wrong" or going ahead without having everything in place. In Viet Nam, for instance, a series of NPM-style managerial devolution measures have been adopted for provincial and lower-level agencies, including one-line budgets, greater flexibility in personnel management and even devolved authority to levy discretionary fees and user charges for government services.[20] At the same time, a portion of successive, substantial across-the-board salary increases must be paid from these local revenues, the rest coming from the central budget.

In sum, the consequences of implementing NPM measures may include some of the following:

- Abolition or downgrading of many central personnel and financial control mechanisms;

- Conversion of civil service departments into free-standing entities, perhaps outside the civil service;

- Performance-based accountability through contracts, replacing old civil service employment rules;

- Deregulation of middle management;

- A strong customer focus in designing and administering services; and

- Extensive use of market-type mechanisms, such as competitive tendering and contracting, both for delivering internal services and for services to the public.[21]

NPM ideas and instruments have added to or refined the store of options available for solving public administration problems, but the result is not a completely new departure that leaves all else behind. In developing countries, it is common to see NPM solutions being applied inappropriately to local problems without at the same time considering all the contingencies and assessing their viability. However, the conclusion should not be drawn that developing countries are not ready for NPM. Rather, a wider array of solutions should be considered for the particular problems in hand, with careful attention to meeting all the requirements for the support systems needed for a particular administrative or management technique.

Labour relations in the public service

As governments gradually moved away from downsizing strategies towards greater appreciation of holistic management of human resources, they realized the need to foster more conducive labour relations in the public sector. This included growing awareness among governments of their special responsibility to consult with staff on changes in working arrangements and to ensure the right of public servants to collective bargaining, as enshrined in the Declaration on Fundamental Principles and Rights at Work of the International Labour Organization (ILO).

Where consultation is concerned, an OECD survey in 2001 revealed that three countries had carried out staff attitude surveys while two more had introduced consultative forums for senior staff. This perspective is also reflected in the recent HRM reform in Canada, which requires departments to set up labour-management consultative committees as a forum for dialogue and discussion on issues of mutual concern. Moreover, there is the evidence from a number of private sector studies that labour-management consultation is generally associated with higher organizational performance, and there seems to be no reason why the public sector should be any different.

Where collective bargaining is concerned, the picture is somewhat complicated. While Italy, New Zealand, Spain and Sweden among the 18 countries in the 2001 OECD study have taken steps to strengthen central collective bargaining, it must be recognized that collective bargaining, even the right to belong to a union, is denied to public servants in many countries. Furthermore, in several others, the unions, which bargain on behalf of public servants, have sometimes been an obstacle to reform. In many countries, unions still mistrust the governments' intentions and the governments assume that unions will be negative while neither troubles to find out the facts.

In Sri Lanka, for example, the management side did not consult the public service unions about its reform programme in the late 1990s. However, one public service union official said that "The government believes we are hostile to reform, but we support reform. If the reform is constructive and in the interests of the country, we support it". In other countries, unions have played a positive role, even in programmes where the prospect of job losses for members has been a real one.

The Civil Servants Association (CSA) of Ghana, for example, was involved in decisions about rightsizing from the beginning through its membership in the Redeployment Management Committee (RMC), which steered the reform process. Far from putting spokes in the wheel, the CSA "gave its blessing", in the words of government officials, even to decisions that would have an adverse impact on its members. Officials were more critical of some of their colleagues in government than the representatives of the CSA. Through its membership in the RMC, the CSA was able to argue for a package of measures such as retraining to alleviate the hardship caused by downsizing.

Similarly, United Kingdom human resource specialists in a National Health Service Trust and in a large local authority took consultations with trade unions seriously. One specialist went so far as to say that the unions were his key change agents and that pushing through job reductions would have been "one hundred times" more difficult without them. In contrast, the Civil Service Union in Uganda was excluded from the relevant steering committee, the Implementation and Monitoring Board, although it had lobbied to be included. It is probably no coincidence that Uganda failed to organize any assistance for retrenched staff other than the redundancy package itself, something which government officials later came to regret bitterly.[22] In a number of countries, unions have also become partners with governments in promoting organizational learning in the public service.

Generally, it seems that ensuring that unions play a positive role is always going to be more difficult in non-competitive markets, such as the public sector. However, dealing successfully with the problems raised by public sector unions will depend on the quality of the legislative framework and the dispute settlement procedures in place. An effective labour legislation for the public sector, for example, would try to set up alternative mechanisms to strikes and lockouts for the settlement of disputes; arbitration by third parties is an obvious example.[23]

It is not only in the public sector that union involvement can be constructive and beneficial. Research in the United Kingdom private sector has discovered that unionized companies are most likely to follow the strategic approach to staff management that is recommended in chapter V of the present report.[24] Thus, governments should, wherever possible, involve public servants and their representatives in staff management decisions in order to respect the rights of employees at work but also to harness their energy to improve efficiency further.

Effective labour management consultation is associated with increased organizational performance

Collective bargaining and unionization are prohibited in many countries

Including unions in reform can pay off, however . . .

. . . the non-competitive environment of the public sector poses a challenge

Diversity management

Those countries that will prosper most in this increasingly globalized world will be those that see diversity as the normal state of affairs, that accept rather than reject other cultures, that understand them, like them, and work with them.

—Tony Blair [25]

Just as with collective bargaining, governments sometimes hesitate to make the workers' "right to be treated equally", enshrined in the ILO Declaration, a reality by taking the necessary steps to protect members of disadvantaged groups, fearing, perhaps, a backlash from more privileged groups or that such steps may be at the expense of efficiency. On the contrary, it is partly because of efficiency—in order to use the stock of human capital in the public service to the fullest—that governments should not ignore the talents of under-represented or under-privileged groups, such as women and certain ethnic, linguistic or religious groups.

Gender imbalance

Evidence from both Israel and Taiwan Province of China shows that organizations that promote and pay women equally tend to be more effective and have lower turnover.[26] Yet sometimes the problem is the lack of a critical mass of talent when it comes to employment in the public service. Among low-income countries, an imbalance in gender distribution is often characteristic of the civil service, partly because fewer girls and young women complete secondary school and university compared with their male counterparts. In some countries, a large imbalance permeates every level of administration as, for instance, in Chad (table 4).

In other countries, female and male civil servants are more or less equally represented. Nevertheless, this does not negate the fact that the composition of these civil services is often skewed in favour of men when it comes to the higher echelons of the administration, as in Argentina and Brazil, for instance. However, the under-representation of women at the higher levels of government is not confined to specific parts of the world. It is a worldwide phenomenon with which developed countries and transition economies in Europe also are grappling, as illustrated in figures 8 and 9.

In general, Eastern European countries have a large representation of women at the higher levels of administration. Remarkably, the Nordic countries do not show a common trend, with only Iceland and Sweden consistently above average.

Low-income countries often have an imbalanced gender distribution in the civil service, . . .

. . . which is also the case at higher levels of government in more developed countries

Table 4.
Composition of Chad's civil service, 2002

Category	Total	Women	Percentage	Men	Percentage
A	4,503	334	7	4,169	93
B	8,340	997	12	7,343	88
C	7,562	1,527	20	6,035	80
D	1,722	175	10	1,547	90
Total	22,127	3,033	14	19,094	86

Source:
Government of Chad, in CAFRAD (2002).[27]

Figure 8.

Decision-makers one level below that of minister in the central administration of 30 European countries, by gender, 2004

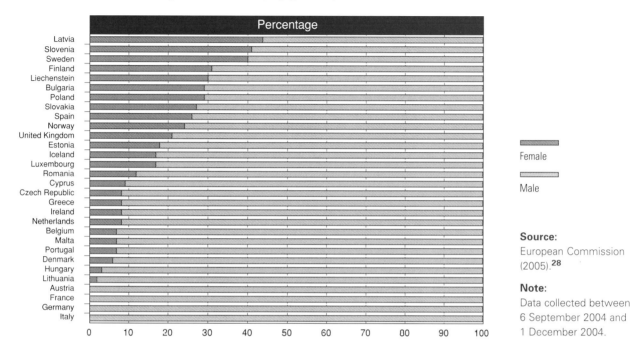

Source:
European Commission (2005).[28]

Note:
Data collected between 6 September 2004 and 1 December 2004.

Figure 9.

Decision-makers two levels below that of minister in the central administration of 30 European countries, by gender, 2004

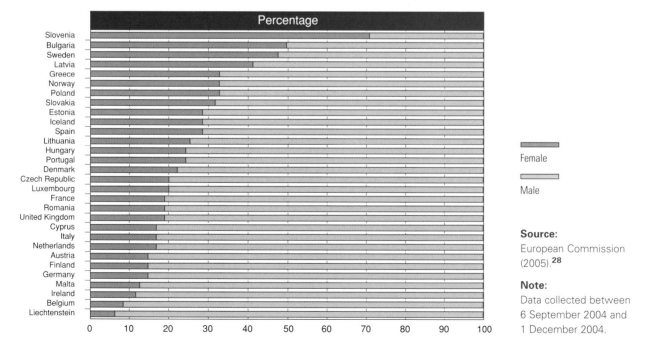

Source:
European Commission (2005).[28]

Note:
Data collected between 6 September 2004 and 1 December 2004.

Accommodating diversity

Accommodating diversity is a necessity primarily on account of the process of diversification present in all societies and organizations. Such growing heterogeneity reflects more than the plurality and visibility of cultures, which must be accommodated in any work place. On a more basic level, heterogeneity springs from the diversity of occupational groups, the product of specialization, which rapid advances in science and technology have left in their wake.

Diversity management is more than affirmative action, . . .

One of the many effects of globalization has been to ease the movement of people across borders and bring them closer together. Proximity, however, has not invariably helped to combat or assuage stereotyping, let alone eliminate prejudice and discrimination. Recent events in the world have brought home to some governments a sense of the diversity of their respective countries and the dangers of exclusion. Nevertheless, it would be an error to view the current emphasis on diversity management purely in terms of "affirmative action", equalizing opportunities or righting historical wrongs, important though these may be.

. . . and it goes well beyond simply maintaining a representative workforce

The emphasis placed by the Government of South Africa on managing diversity was dictated largely by the awareness of its strategic importance to socio-economic development as well as the desire to promote a high level of efficiency and productivity in the public service. The Government decided that in order to correct the imbalances of the past, the issue of management of diversity had to be addressed at the highest level (i.e., the national constitution). The Constitution specifies that "Public administration must be broadly representative of the South African people, with employment and personnel management practices based on ability, objectivity, fairness, and the need to redress the imbalances of the past to achieve broad representation".[29] In presenting the case for managing diversity, however, the Government of South Africa strongly noted that the need to develop a culture of diversity goes well beyond simply maintaining a representative workforce.

There are also a number of business-related arguments in favour of diversity management, including the following:

- *Contribution to improved service delivery.* Developing a more responsive, customer-focused approach to the recipients of public services requires public servants who are able to relate to every section of South Africa's society, familiarity with the needs of citizens and an ability to both communicate with and respond to their concerns.

- *Fresh thinking, innovative approaches and new ideas.* Meeting the challenges facing the public service will require fresh thinking and innovative approaches, often outside the traditional public service culture. Encouraging diversity of culture can generate new ideas and get them adopted.

- *Morale, job satisfaction and increased productivity.* A culture of equality where different member groups are valued is likely to boost staff morale and contribute to increased job satisfaction and thus to increased productivity.

South Africa is a concrete example of how a government can act to eliminate discrimination and promote the participation of disadvantaged groups while drafting legislation sensitively in order to ensure that efficiency is not eroded. Given the history of institutionalized discrimination against non-white citizens in South Africa, both the 1993 and the 1996 constitutions contain a non-discrimination clause with sufficient teeth to be invoked successfully in the High Court, as in the ironic case of a white state government lawyer unfairly passed over for promotion in 1995. Significantly, in interpreting the legislators' intentions, "The Court found it difficult to believe that the legislature intended that a more representative civil service should be created at the cost of qualifications, expertise and experience".[30]

The Constitution, however, recognizing that non-white groups had been "historically disadvantaged" because of the legacy of "apartheid", also allowed for positive affirmative action measures. In 1998, the Government published the *White Paper on Affirmative Action in the Public Service,* aimed at addressing disadvantage while affirming the complementary importance of providing good public services. The much-touted model of the Indian Administrative Service, with its efforts to reach out to all segments of Indian society, has also shown interesting adaptive capabilities in face of modern pressures. Initiatives in both South Africa and India reflect their unique history and experiences, but they are echoed by similar, albeit less wide-ranging, initiatives in a number of rich countries, notably Australia, Canada, Denmark, France, Iceland, Norway and Spain.

Notes

1 Nunberg, Barbara (1997). *Rethinking Civil Service Reform: An Agenda for Smart Government.* Poverty and Social Policy Working Paper. Washington, D.C.: World Bank.

2 The Economist (1998). Zhu takes on the red-tape army. *The Economist,* vol. 45 (United Kingdom, 83). 14 March.

3 Organisation for Economic Co-operation and Development (1994). Public management developments. Paris: OECD.

4 Kiragu, Kithinji (2002). Improving Service Delivery through Public Service Reform: Lessons of Experience from Selected Sub-Saharan Africa Countries. Development Assistance Committee Network on Good Governance and Capacity Development. Paris: OECD.

5 Lienert, Ian (1998). Civil service reform in Africa: mixed results after 10 years. *Finance and Development,* vol. 35, no. 2 (June). Available from http://www.imf.org/external/pubs/ft/fandd/1998/06/lienert.htm

6 Adamolekun, Ladipo (2002). Africa's evolving career civil service systems: three challenges—state continuity, efficient service delivery and accountability. *International Review of Administrative Sciences,* vol. 68, issue 3, p. 381.

7 Therkildsen, Ole (2001). Efficiency, accountability and implementation: public sector reform in East and Southern Africa. United Nations Research Institute for Social Development.

8 Organisation for Economic Co-operation and Development (2001). *Recent Developments on Human Resources Management in OECD Member Countries.* Public Management Committee. Paris: OECD.

9 Municipality of Copenhagen. Press releases: 13 June 2003, 29 September 2004 and 11 February 2005; and Thomas Flensburg (2005). Municipality of Copenhagen found guilty in payroll chaos. *Politiken.* 7 February.

10 Hood, C., C. Scott, O. James, G. Jones and T. Travers (1999). *Regulation inside Government: Waste-Watchers, Quality Police and Sleaze-Busters.* Oxford: Oxford University Press.

11 Ingraham, Patricia W. (1999). Of pigs in pokes and policy diffusion: another look at pay-for-performance. *Public Administration Review,* vol. 53, no. 4 (Jul.–Aug.), pp. 348–356; and Michael Katula and James L. Perry (2003). Comparative performance pay. In *Handbook of Public Administration,* B. Guy Peters and Jon Pierre, eds. London: Sage Publications, pp. 53–61.

12 Government of the Republic of Korea (2001). *How Korea Reformed the Public Sector.* Seoul: Ministry of Planning and Budget.

13 Christensen, Tom and Per Laegreid (2001). A transformative perspective on administrative reforms. In *New Public Management: the Transformation of Ideas and Practice,* Christensen and Legreid, eds. Aldershot: Ashgate.

14 Evans, Peter (2004). Development as institutional change: the pitfalls of monocropping and the potentials of deliberation. *Studies in Comparative International Development,* vol. 38, issue 4 (winter), p. 32.

15   Tendler, Judith (1998). *Good Government in the Tropics*. Baltimore, MD: Johns Hopkins University Press.

16   Schick, Allen (1998). Why most developing countries should not try New Zealand's reforms. *World Bank Research Observer*, vol. 13, issue 1, pp. 129–130.

17   Manning, Nick (2001). The legacy of the new public management in developing countries. *International Review of Administrative Sciences*, vol. 67, issue 2, p. 303.

18   Tendler, Judith (1998). Op. cit.

19   Polidano, Charles (1999). *The New Public Management in Developing Countries*. Working Paper No. 13. Institute for Development Policy and Management. Manchester: University of Manchester, pp. 27–28.

20   Painter, Martin (2004). Hybrids, varietals and foreign bodies: public service salary reform in Vietnam. 20th Anniversary Conference of the Structure and Organization of Government Research Committee of the International Political Science Association. Vancouver, June 15–17. Available from http://www.politics.ubc.ca/campbell/sog-conf/papers/sog2004-painter.pdf

21   Polidano, Charles (1999). *The New Public Management in Developing Countries*. Working Paper No. 13. Institute for Development Policy and Management. Manchester: University of Manchester, p. 2.

22   McCourt, Willy (2001). Towards a strategic model of employment reform: explaining and remedying experience to date. *International Journal of Human Resource Management*, vol. 12, issue 1, pp. 56–75.

23   World Bank (1995). *World Development Report: A Better Investment Climate for Everyone*. Washington, D.C.: World Bank.

24   Guest, David E. and Riccardo Peccei (2001). Partnership at work: mutuality and the balance of advantage, *British Journal of Industrial Relations*, vol. 39, issue 2, pp. 207–236.

25   Blair, Tony, Prime Minister, United Kingdom (2000). Speech delivered at the Network's Annual General Meeting. 28 November. Available from http://www.number-10.gov.uk/output/Page1550.asp

26   Bowen, Chieh-Chen (2003). Sex discrimination in selection and compensation in Taiwan. *International Journal of Human Resource Management*, vol. 14, issue 2, pp. 297–315; and G. Harel, S. Tzafrir and Y. Baruch (2003). Achieving organizational effectiveness through promotion of women into managerial positions: HRM practice focus. *International Journal of Human Resource Management*, vol. 14, issue 2, pp. 247–263.

27   African Training and Research Centre in Administration for Development (CAFRAD) (2002). Questionnaire on National Public Administrations in Africa. Tangier, Morocco: CAFRAD.

28   European Commission (2005). Database on women and men in decision-making. Directorate General for Employment, Social Affairs and Equal Opportunities. Data collected between 6 Sep. 2004 and 1 Dec. 2004. Available from http://europa.eu.int/comm/employment_social/women_men_stats/index_en.htm

29   Constitution of the Republic of South Africa (1996). Section 195 (1).

30   Government of South Africa (1998). *White Paper on Affirmative Action*. Pretoria: Department of Public Service and Administration.

Chapter V
Managing people as a strategic resource

Adopting a holistic approach to reform

What actions should governments take to manage their staff better? The present chapter discusses some of the key elements of a strategic approach to HRM reform in the public sector. The report recommends that governments consider the development of an HRM strategy that builds on the best attributes of three broad models or schools in public administration: traditional public administration; public management, including NPM; and responsive governance. Each one of the three models has particular strengths and highlights core values that are relevant to address contemporary HRM challenges in the public sector.

Interestingly, some of the early and most enthusiastic adopters of the NPM model, such as Australia and New Zealand, have in recent years rediscovered the virtues of traditional public administration, in particular, the value of the principles of impartiality and merit. The public management model has also contributed important principles, tools and techniques to HRM reform, particularly in the area of performance and results-based management. And recently, the governance paradigm has brought to the fore new approaches and concepts to make public administration more responsive to the demands of citizens and other stakeholders. Each model therefore offers important attributes that can be harnessed to improve HRM in the public sector. The report suggests that the unifying principles of such an HRM synthesis could be *impartiality, professionalism* and *responsiveness.*

As the starting point for the development of a synthetic HRM framework for the civil service, the following components were identified in chapter I:

- A politically impartial, professional and merit-based civil service;

- A core "guardian" agency, exercising strategic leadership and monitoring a system of dispersed management rather than operating through bureaucratic controls;

- A strong focus on results-oriented management in the public service through the use of effective performance standards and indicators as well as promotion criteria giving greater weight to relative efficiency (rather than relying only on seniority);

- Tough, objective anti-corruption rules and agencies;

- Legislative provisions and professional norms that facilitate making the civil service open to external scrutiny; and

- Systems and skill sets that provide high levels of communication capacity through being networked by the effective deployment of information technology.

The above-mentioned components are intended to serve only as an illustration of how governments can develop an HRM synthesis that meets their own specific needs and priorities in order to fully harness the ability of staff to contribute to the achievement of national development goals. The HRM synthesis is a guidepost, something for governments to compare

Wholesale overnight reform based on a blueprint rarely occurs themselves against, rather than a blueprint. Wholesale overnight reform based on a blueprint rarely occurs and is probably undesirable even where it does, as discussed in chapter II.

Table 5 highlights selected HRM features of the three models. While the report advocates that developing countries would be well advised to put in place first a well-functioning career-based civil service before embarking on more complex legal and institutional reform, there are many possibilities of revitalizing civil service management by selectively infusing features of the public management and responsive governance models into traditional public administration.

Governments that have put in place a traditional public administration system, for example, can make it more responsive by adopting measures such as the following: subjecting senior officials to 360-degree accountability; strengthening performance measurement and reporting; introducing organizational learning into the public service; re-focusing on values that promote citizen-centred delivery of services; and strengthening labour-management relations. Such incremental but strategic reform measures can undoubtedly make a difference in enhancing the responsiveness of the public service to various stakeholders in society without undermining the core tenets of traditional public administration.

In the same vein, governments can enhance the professionalism of the public service by infusing some of the best features of the public management model into traditional

Table 5.
Selected HRM features of the three models of public administration

	Public administration	**Public management**	**Responsive governance**
Civil service system	Closed and bounded	Open and decentralized	Open and regulated
	Career civil service	Position-based system	Core career civil service; other posts position-based
	Tenure	Fixed-term	Tenure and fixed-term
Institutional arrangements	Independent central personnel authority	HRM decentralized to line ministries	Lead HRM regulator; decentralized HRM
	Personnel administration	Human resource management	Strategic HRM and development
	Unified pay system	Individual contracts	Unified and performance-based pay system
Career advancement	Seniority-based	Performance-based	Range of competencies
Pay policy	Qualifications and experience-based	Job-based criteria with performance element	Job-based criteria with performance element
Performance management	Professional ethics	Performance agreement	360-degree accountability
Human resource development	Functional skills	Competencies	Competencies and relational skills

administration. This may include greater emphasis on the professionalization of HRM, including integration of staff management into strategic organizational planning processes in the public service; recalibration of the pay policy to better link it to underlying labour market conditions; introduction of competency-based staff selection and training; and setting service quality standards in the public sector.

Whatever components governments identify as priorities for their respective HRM synthesis, they would generally be well advised to follow a holistic, yet gradual, approach to HRM reform in the public sector. In an ideal world, governments would work through the items of a holistic framework in a logical order. However, in keeping with the notion of "starting from where you find yourself", a government may choose, for example, to begin with performance management as a way of making managers aware, for the first time, that they are responsible for the performance of staff, as Morocco did; or with job reduction because of an overriding need to bring spending on staff into line with government income, as Cambodia and many other developing countries and transition economies have done; or, indeed, with any human resource issue that is a current priority.

HRM reform should be holistic yet gradual
The entry point for HRM reform will always differ from one country to the next

Building an effective HRM institutional framework

Legal and regulatory reform

Traditionally, the primary objective of laws and regulations governing public servants has been to shield staff from political, ethnic, religious and fiscal interference as well as to protect the public from an arbitrary, or even biased, delivery of services and administration. Apart from stipulating which functions should be granted civil service status (an ever-contentious issue), laws and regulations, importantly, define the role of the civil service in the management of public affairs and the values and principles that should guide civil servants in the exercise of their duties, and establish their rights and obligations.

Some of the most comprehensive reforms of legal frameworks in the public sector in recent years have taken place in the former Eastern bloc countries. In the Soviet era, civil servants in these countries were subject to ordinary labour law. The break-up of the Eastern bloc, however, spurred major administrative and civil service reform. Initially, civil services were primarily reorganized in accordance with employment models based on private law before statutory mechanisms were adopted in the late 1990s and the early years of the new century.[1] The latter development, in particular, was facilitated by the prospect of accession of many former Eastern bloc countries to the European Union.

Comprehensive reform has taken place in the former Eastern bloc countries

At the same time, several developing countries have opted to confine the status of civil servants to the core bodies of government while relying on more flexible employment arrangements to manage, for instance, teachers in the educational sector. Yet in developed countries, the purviews of statutes are often long established. Thus, with continuity ensured, the main aim of reform has generally been to introduce greater flexibility into "how" public policy goals are achieved. In some cases, this has led to greater use of fixed-term employment contracts in the public service, particularly when it has been deemed important to recalibrate staff competencies in priority sectors in order to make the public service workforce more responsive to the needs of citizens.

Whether governments need to establish or amend legislation governing civil service employment, the present report advocates that embedding the principle of merit is essential.

Even though various forces have coalesced to complement how merit is ascertained or balanced with other values, such as diversity and representation, the traditional definition and application of merit are still valid but may in many instances need to be modernized. The development of a modern definition of what constitutes a merit-based career civil service should be accorded priority in many developing countries.

The 2003 Public Service Modernization Act in Canada is an example of how merit can be determined by law. Previously, merit in the Canadian civil service was defined through case law and precedent, which resulted in a process-driven appointment regime. Historically, merit meant selecting the best-qualified person among applicants. This changed with the Public Service Employment Act (PSEA) in 1992, where merit was broadened to also include measuring qualifications against a set of standards. The recent changes brought about by the 2003 Act are described in Box 11.

The promotion of integrity is of equal importance in the public service. It is not hard to identify the institutional arrangements that most successfully promote integrity and combat corruption. First, there should be a coherent set of laws with criminal, civil and administrative legal provisions that penalize corruption in the public service. These provisions should be clear and impose sufficient penalties to serve as a deterrent and a basis for enforcement. In the case of

Coherent laws which penalize corruption are a prerequisite

Box 11

The Public Service Modernization Act—Canada

The principles of non-partisanship and merit have always been fundamental to the vision of the Canadian public service. Merit is the basis for all appointments in the public service. However, the term has never been articulated in legislation and has therefore been defined mainly through case law and precedent. This lack of a clear definition of what constitutes merit has resulted in a very cumbersome, process-driven appointment regime, which has inhibited the ability of the public service to recruit and promote staff effectively.

The public service in Canada, as elsewhere, is facing many human resource management (HRM) challenges, including an increasingly competitive labour market; demographic changes in terms of both age and representation; the growing need to invest in staff development, to improve labour-management relations and to sharpen accountability lines; and the gradual deterioration in the image of public sector employment, which has made it more difficult for managers to recruit and retain talent.

Against this backdrop, the Parliament of Canada adopted in November 2003 the Public Service Modernization Act (PSMA). The Act, which will come into full force in mid to late 2005, will bring about the biggest changes in HRM in Canada in more than 35 years. It consists of four pieces of legislation: the Public Service Employment Act; the Public Service Labour Relations Act; Amendments to the Financial Administration Act; and Amendments to the Canadian Centre for Management Development Act. The new law also establishes the Public Service Human Resources Management Agency of Canada, which is charged with the implementation of the HRM reform agenda.

The PSMA aims to achieve four main objectives:

• Make the staffing regime more flexible to facilitate hiring the right people when and where they are needed with built-in safeguards;

• Foster more collaborative labour-management relations;

• Promote more focused, better-integrated learning and training of employees at all levels; and

• Articulate more clearly the roles and responsibilities of the Treasury Board Secretariat, the Public Service Commission, Deputy Heads and their managers.

The PSMA reinforces safeguards to sustain merit-based, non-partisan public service rooted in the values of transparency, fairness and respect. Deputy Heads will continue to be able to set the qualifications for the work that must be performed within their respective organizations, and once the PSMA is fully implemented, managers will have greater flexibility in the area of staffing. The PSMA also establishes a Public Service Staffing Tribunal to resolve disputes between staff and management. The Public Service Commission will continue to play a critical role in protecting the integrity of government-wide hiring processes. The PSMA will also require departments to set up labour-management consultation committees as a forum for dialogue on issues of mutual concern. In addition, the PSMA will promote lifelong learning and career development. The Canada School of Public Service will be open and accessible to employees at all levels in departments, agencies and all regions.

That the Government of Canada was able to enact such far-reaching reform is largely a result of strong support among political and administrative leaders and other key stakeholders. There was consensus on the need to significantly strengthen HRM in the public service, which made the adoption of the draft law politically feasible. As a result, parliamentary debate on the draft law was vigorous, and union leaders, academics and former and current public service executives offered their knowledge and expertise during the committee hearings. The preparatory process also involved extensive consultations with public servants.

Source:
See Bibliography.

bureaucratic corruption, they should include both a set of internal disciplinary measures that, among other things, can result in dismissal and loss of pension rights and designated administrative units to carry them out. Second, administrative rules and procedures should be clear and transparent to inform citizens of their rights, responsibilities and standards of service. Such transparency, followed by accountability of public servants for their performance, favours citizen and business engagement and serves as an effective measure to promote professionalism and curbing of corruption. To facilitate public feedback, avenues of public complaint and redress should also be made available.

In sum, a clear legal framework is the indispensable foundation for HRM in the public sector. The framework should provide continuity in the management of staff yet at the same time provide adequate flexibility for the government of the day to modernize the application of key principles and concepts, as required by the demands of the evolving public sector environment. When drafting legislation, governments should at least pay attention to the following key questions:[2]

- Which possible policy option is preferred?
- Should this option be realized through legislation rather than by non-legislative means?
- Which authorities should put the legislation into effect?
- What is the basic approach to be adopted in the legislation?
- What legal and administrative mechanisms are necessary to put that approach into effect and make it workable?

Because of the strategic role of civil servants in maintaining state institutions over time, statutory or some other form of institutional protection is necessary, particularly in developing countries. In an impartial, professional and responsive civil service, the appointed officials must also be subordinate to the politicians whom the people have elected. At the same time, it is also appropriate to distinguish the political from the administrative sphere.

Politicians should "steer but not row"

Broadly speaking, politicians should "steer but not row": establish the policy framework, set targets where necessary, but then let the officials get on with the job of implementing the policy and meeting the targets in a professional and responsive manner. For their part, officials should implement policies faithfully, within reason, and not seek to create a rival power base.

It may also be necessary to specify the remit of basic institutions in the national Constitution, and to amend the Constitution when those institutions have proved to be inadequate. The experience of Sri Lanka exemplifies this well. In 1972, the Government removed the independence of the Public Service Commission (PSC), the body responsible for civil service staffing, placing it under the Cabinet in an attempt to make civil servants less remote from citizens and more responsive to development objectives. This, however, led to the politicization of public appointments and deterioration in the quality of the public service. In 2001, in a remarkable exercise in self-denial, all the major parties united to support a constitutional amendment that restored the independence of the PSC. They also consented to the appointment of commissioners who were determined to make that independence a reality even if it meant standing up to politicians.

Central government: *assigning the HRM leadership role*

When governments discuss where to put responsibility for human resource management, they often do so in terms of how much authority the centre should have relative to line departments and agencies. However, governments also need to decide on the appropriate division of responsibility between the central departments and agencies themselves. In many of the countries that have not devolved HRM responsibility to line ministries and agencies, the respective roles of government ministries look broadly like those in table 6.

This structure is particularly close to the Commonwealth model, especially with respect to the role of the Public Service Commission (PSC), but even non-Commonwealth countries such as the Republic of Korea and Thailand have a similar arrangement in place. PSCs are often attributed to the Westminster model, while in most francophone countries, the responsibilities of the PSC are generally devolved to individual ministries, approximating the mixed French system.

One important element that this idealized version omits is the organization of public servants in many countries into cadres or corps, each with its own parent ministry. For the most part, cadres and ministries correspond fairly closely. Thus, most members of the education

Potential conflict exists for cadre personnel

Table 6.
Responsibility for HRM in central government agencies

Agency	Function
Office of the Prime Minister	Overall government policy
Ministry of Finance	Pay and pensions
Ministry of Public Service	Deployment and conditions of service for public servants
Public Service Commission	Appointment, promotion, transfer and discipline
National Administrative Staff College	Training and development

corps work in schools, under the authority of the Ministry of Education. However, members of the administrative cadre may be posted to any ministry even though their promotion and transfer are nominally controlled by the Ministry of Public Service. This creates the potential for conflict between the "parent" ministry and the ministry in which the administrator actually works.

It is easy to see how this structure can lead to a fragmentation of HRM from a strategic point of view and to its being a source of conflict among the different agencies. In the structural adjustment era when many governments were trying to reduce staff numbers, Ministries of Public Service were often seen by their finance counterparts as a Trojan horse inside government, acting as an informal trade union to frustrate the aims of reform.[3] Thus, staff in the Ministry of Finance in Ghana, for example, made no secret of their view that their counterparts in the Ministry of Public Service were the biggest single threat to the success of reform.[4]

Ministries of Public Service are sometimes seen as a Trojan horse

Again from a strategic HRM point of view, the remedy would appear to be simple: bring all these functions together in a single strategic agency, possibly the Office of the Prime Minister or something similar. Some governments have moved in this direction. It was part of the reason why the Government of the United Kingdom abolished the Ministry for the Civil Service in 1979 and moved its responsibilities into the Cabinet Office. There is probably no government that has taken that argument to its logical conclusion, however. In particular, ministries of finance everywhere are reluctant to surrender their power over the pay of public servants, which consumes a large proportion of public expenditure.

Strategic HRM functions should be brought together in a single agency

The path-dependent character of public administration, discussed in chapter II, is another reason why well-established bodies with a tradition of competence, such as national administrative staff colleges, retain their pivotal position even though their very existence weakens the strategic thrust of government.

The universal lesson is that the principles underlying an impartial, professional, and responsive public service need to be institutionalized, promulgated and protected by a prestigious, powerful guardian agency (or set of agencies) at the centre of government. Such an agency should aim at promoting and replicating a set of values and behaviours through guidance and advice on civil service employment policy; developing ethical codes; and exercising special oversight of recruitment, promotion and performance appraisal of civil servants and career planning for senior levels of the core civil service.

A guardian agency at the central level is necessary to promulgate unified values and principles

The lead government agency for HRM would often be the Office of the Prime Minister and, in some cases, the Ministry of Public Service or its equivalent. The coordinating agency needs to put into place a suitable structure for consulting other central agencies—and possibly also line ministries—in order to develop an HRM policy. In recent years, the Ministry for the Civil Service in Morocco has held occasional *tables rondes* (round tables), bringing together representatives from a large number of agencies. Such an initiative is a useful first step towards setting up a more regular coordinating structure.

Coordination requires consultation and participation

Central and line agencies: *establishing the division of HRM responsibility*

Devolution of management responsibility to line agencies is a central part of the new public management (NPM) formula for managing public services, and it is reflected in the practice of many industrialized countries. In the United Kingdom Civil Service, for example, delegation has been a gradual process that began in 1964 when the recruitment of clerical staff was devolved to departments. The central Civil Service Commission still continued to approve appointments, but the need to seek approval disappeared in 1983. In 1991, all recruitment

With strategy at the centre, devolution of HRM responsibilities enhances performance . . .

below Grade 7 (a middle-management level) was also devolved, and in 1995, the cut-off point was further raised to Grade 5 (a senior-management level).

In addition, the centre has progressively delegated power over pay and grading to departments. The role of the United Kingdom Civil Service Commission is now merely to issue standards of conduct, make appointments down to Grade 5, hear appeals, commission selection audits and promote best practice within departments by issuing guidelines on selection. Within United Kingdom line agencies, managers are responsible for selection, discipline, performance rewards and career development. HRM units have come into their own as contributors to departmental personnel strategies and policies and providers of support services to line managers. These units are responsible for pay and ranking below Grade 5, succession planning, auditing and monitoring line performance, and providing advice on selection, discipline and training when managers need it. Thus, after a full quarter century of gradual devolution, the idea of a uniform, centrally managed civil service is coming to an end in the United Kingdom. It is professional peer pressure rather than central controls that now maintains the integrity of staffing in the public service.

Devolution may be appropriate, however, in countries that implement it gradually and where the mechanism of professional peer pressure is able to operate. In countries where containing nepotism and favouritism is a priority, improving recruitment quality and responsiveness is best dealt with through a central staffing structure, as reflected in the two-stage model of reform outlined in chapter II. In fact, in countries where respect for the rule of law and a culture of transparency are not ingrained, where, on the contrary, nepotism and favouritism are rampant, effective central control may be the only viable option.

Increasingly, as governments have begun to question the value of the NPM model, there has been an acknowledgement that too rapid decentralization of HRM functions may lead to a decline in the professionalism of the core civil service. The diminution of the role of the central personnel agencies with their service-wide responsibilities has also meant that some significant support systems for the maintenance of the civil service ethos have been neglected.

Box 12

The role of ICTs in facilitating decentralized HRM—Cameroon

Prior to 2002, the management of state personnel in Cameroon was centralized in two ministries: the Ministry of Public Service and Administrative Reform (MINFOPRA) for career development of staff, and the Ministry of Finance and Budget (MINFIB) for pay and pension. This management arrangement, however, had gradually resulted in significant delays in the processing of staff records; weak accountability for both individual and organizational performance; and the swelling of the wage bill, owing to poor mechanisms for verifying the actual number of staff.

The centralized nature of the personnel management system also meant that other ministries, while responsible for the work performed by the respective staff, had little or no say in matters relating to promotion, advancement or penalty in case of poor performance. It was also very difficult to determine with accuracy the total number of state employees, with conflicting figures coming from MINFOPRA and MINFIB, creating uncertainty for the wage bill.

The Government therefore decided to embark on a new programme to strengthen HRM in the public sector. An important part of the reform agenda was to devolve HRM to the ministry level. To facilitate this process, the Government developed the integrated computerized state personnel and payroll management system, known by its French acronym SIGIPES, as the hub for all personnel and

Box 12 (cont'd)

payroll-related information in the public service. The system has since been piloted in four ministries: MINFIB, MINFOPRA, the Ministry of Education, and the Ministry of Health.

As a result of SIGIPES, senior managers in government now have access to up-to-date information concerning pay and personnel. In addition, the system provides government employees with online access to the status of personal inquiries pertaining to matters such as selection, promotion, training and retirement. Senior managers in MINFOPRA can also access the data in SIGIPES to ensure that proper procedures are being followed by staff managing the system. By making government procedures more transparent and by reducing the need for interaction between clerks and clients, the efficiency and transparency of HRM have increased and opportunities for corruption have been reduced. This has been one of the key benefits of SIGIPES. The effective implementation of the system is also attributed to the security of the data circulating through the system, the quality of both hardware and software solutions, and the quality of the training of the officials involved in its operation.

A major factor explaining the success of SIGIPES has been the step-by-step approach to its implementation taken by MINFOPRA coupled with accurate information and complete transparency. In 2004, MINFOPRA was awarded a United Nations Public Service Award for SIGIPES. As the result of its successful pilot phase, the use of SIGIPES is now being expanded to other ministries in Cameroon.

Sources:
See Bibliography.

More recently, as discussed in chapter IV, the emphasis on deregulation of HRM functions has been criticized for imposing new, more burdensome constraints on managers because of its unintended consequences. In the United Kingdom, abolition of central personnel controls and the creation of autonomous agencies within the civil service were accompanied by new forms of regulation that led to an increase in the number of regulators and a growing trend towards codifying previously unwritten norms and conventions.[5]

> Deregulation has led to the codifying of previously unwritten norms and conventions

Together, these developments have highlighted the need for a balanced approach to HRM reform, such as recommended by participants at a UN/DESA workshop, "Building the Human Capital in the Public Sector", held at the Fifth Global Forum on Reinventing Government (Mexico, November 2003). The meeting concluded that "while the delegation of recruitment of staff from central agencies . . . has generally proved effective, the existence of adequate oversight and quality control mechanisms in this area is essential to avoid abuses and malpractices".[6] This remains a key organizational challenge for governments, including those that have gone down the NPM path.

Professionalizing human resource management

HRM units: *towards strategic specialization*

Our lessons learned showed a need for more collective and horizontal approaches to all aspects of managing the Public Service. This is reinforced by the fact that people are the critical capital of a modern, knowledge-based organization. As we are faced with competition for knowledge-workers in an environment where significant retirements are anticipated for private and public sector organizations, a strategic plan is required for future success.

—Government of Canada[7]

Every government needs to develop a policy statement that defines how staff management will contribute to the achievement of its overall strategic objectives. This statement will not

Every government
needs a strategy
on how staff will
contribute to its
overall goals

change overnight—an intrinsic characteristic of strategy is that it is not easily reversible—but it is likely to change when a new party with its own objectives or "manifesto" (to use the language of politics) comes to power. Indeed, it may change even if the governing party is returned to power following an election to the extent that the party presented a new manifesto to the electorate in order to win a fresh mandate. To be of any value, a strategy must be seen as important; it must not be easily reversible; and it must involve the commitment of government resources over a significant period.[8] The time and effort lavished on it are justified only if it is not automatically discarded every time a government changes hands.

Strategy must be
comprehensive
and consistent

A strategy must be comprehensive and consistent. From the mid-1990s onwards, South Africa's Department of Public Service and Administration worked out very detailed blueprints to give flesh to its ambition to "transform" the public service from a command-and-control bureaucracy to an instrument for providing services to citizens. Often, however, public HRM strategy, just as in the private sector, can be piecemeal and emergent. An example is Botswana's strategic decision in the late 1990s to become a pay "follower" rather than "leader", that is, to follow the pay norms that were evolving in the private sector rather than to set its own pay rates in some rational but isolated way. In either case, the government needs to recognize the enormous benefits of managing its staff strategically so that they are contributing to achieving the government's overall political and development objectives.

The HRM function is
commonly discharged
by generalists

Whatever HRM strategy a government chooses to adopt, it will need to provide professional HRM support to the managers who make staffing decisions. Such support is necessary because those decisions are complex and there is a body of professional good practice that will enable managers to make them in a better way. Nevertheless, while many governments have professional, and sometimes very prestigious, cadres or corps in some areas, with members who include graduates of elite academies such as France's *École nationale d'administration* (National School of Public Administration), the HRM function is commonly discharged by generalist administrators, often coming under an administrative cadre, corps or similar structure.

In the early 1990s, a study of the way that governments managed their staff in three African countries—Kenya, United Republic of Tanzania and Zimbabwe—found that staff responsible for human resources played a restricted, bureaucratic and reactive role, confined by and large to routine decisions about staff entitlement to pay increments and the like, very many of which could be "read" off the administrative regulations governing staff behaviour. They had little or no real input into strategic decisions about staff management, let alone decisions on how to achieve the overall core objectives of government. The study noted that this style of HRM derived from three factors:

- The "cult of the generalist", which the independent governments had inherited from the former colonial powers, whereby HRM was seen as a simple, non-professional aspect of general administration;

- The inflexible, centralized approach to staff management discussed earlier, which was designed to contain the ever-present incidence of favouritism and corruption by restricting the discretion of line agencies and managers; and

- The absence of alternative HRM models and HRM specialists.[9]

More recent studies have shown that this narrow role remains especially widespread in developing states, and not only in the above-mentioned African countries.

Which model of the HRM function will best enable governments to manage their staff so as to achieve their key objectives? One widely accepted model for an organization where it is line managers who take day-to-day staffing decisions—referred to here as "strategic specialization"—outlines the following roles:

- *Strategy expert:* the strategic HRM role;

- *Work organization expert:* the professional role where HRM staff are experts on activities such as selection and training and are able to advise line managers on how to design a selection procedure or a training course and so on;

- *Employee champion:* the "spokesperson" role, relaying employees' concerns about working conditions to senior managers (for example, a concern that a downsizing programme will unreasonably increase the workload of the staff who stay behind); and

- *Agent of continuous transformation:* the organization development role, acting as an adviser on change management processes, such as the stages that a public agency should go through when it implements a skills development programme.[10]

Staff who play these roles will need to be specialists, advisers, consultants or business partners. They will need to have both a solid understanding of the environment in which the organization operates and the ability to deliver services efficiently. The typical career trajectory of the generalist public servant, who may previously have been a district officer and who can expect to become the chairman of a statutory board later on, is inadequate. Governments will need to invest in the training of their own administrators or appoint HRM specialists from the outside, if needed, in order to manage the staff effectively. HRM specialists also need to be taken seriously by senior officials and politicians if they aspire to influence the strategic management of human resources in the public sector.

Staff discharging HRM functions need to be specialists

Competence frameworks: *setting the standard for performance*

It is my hope that competencies will provide us with shared language for talking, in concrete terms, about high performance and managerial excellence. I believe that a shared view of the standards we are striving to achieve will assist us in our continuing efforts to prepare the Organization to meet the challenges of the 21st century.

—Kofi Annan[11]

The application of an integrated competence-based model is important to good HRM practice in the public service. By promoting a consistent approach across all HRM activities, the framework helps to ensure that the management of human resources contributes effectively to achieving the government's objectives (sometimes called "vertical integration") and ensuring that the HRM whole is greater than the sum of the individual activities (sometimes called "horizontal integration"). An important objective in the development of such frameworks in the public service is to promote a shared language as it relates to performance standards and expectations.

An integrated competence-based model is important for good HRM practice

Managers and staff need to learn to discuss both expectations and actual performance

Table 7.
A competence framework for HRM

HRM Activity	Use of competence model
Merit-based appointment	Acts as "person specification" framework to give criteria for selection
Pay and rewards	Used in "job evaluation" to give basis for pay and grading
Performance management	Provides framework for managing staff performance
Job reduction	Helps government to identify priority jobs and jobs that are no longer needed
Human resource development	Enables managers and jobholders to identify "performance gap" between existing competence and job requirements

A competence framework developed by the Irish Civil Service illustrates this idea. Its authors point out that "When we talk about developing competencies we mean the development of the necessary behaviours and attributes as well as knowledge and skills required to do our jobs well in a way in which we realise our potential and provide the highest quality service to our customers".[12] The Irish model places the competency framework at the centre of civil service management. The framework describes seventeen behavioural competencies, which have been identified as relevant in the current civil service environment. Once such a framework has been developed, it can be used across a range of HRM activities (table 7).

Human resource development provides an example of this use. A competence framework similar to the one used in the Irish Civil Service has been employed at INTAN, the civil service staff training college in Malaysia, as a basis for developing the management skills of senior officials. In such a training programme, officials are asked to state whether particular competences constitute a strong or weak area for them. If they feel that a particular competence is an area that they need to develop, they are asked to state which steps they will take to do so.

It should be noted that a competence framework can be used in both public agencies that appoint staff from outside to quite senior positions ("lateral entry") and agencies that promote from within. In the former system, competencies can be the basis for such appointments from outside; but equally in the latter system, competencies offer the criteria for developing the internally appointed person who may need skills for the new position—skills that were not acquired earlier in the person's career.

Merit-based appointment: *getting the best person for the job*

The natural aristocracy [the grounds of which are virtue and talents] I consider as the most precious gift of nature for the instruction, the trusts, and government of society.
—Thomas Jefferson[13]

A meritocratic civil service is of universal importance to performance

As highlighted in chapter II, a merit-oriented, career-based civil service is a key factor in explaining public sector performance. Several studies have corroborated this and have also attributed economic growth and poverty reduction to the institutional features of merit-based appointment and career stability.[14] While building meritocratic civil service is of universal importance to performance,[15] it also means tapping into talent in under-represented groups to ensure that the public service adequately represents all relevant segments of society, as discussed in chapter IV.

Merit can be defined as "the appointment of the best person for any given job"; it is the thrust of the French Napoleonic ideal of *"une carrière ouverte aux talents"*. Thus, in a pure merit system, all public appointments, from top to bottom, are made following a competition based on merit rules that are publicly understood and can be challenged if a breach is suspected. While the definition itself is trite and uncontroversial, there are four situations where the application of the merit principle runs counter to the practice of many administrations.

Exceptions to merit and competitive recruitment

Probably no administration operates a pure merit or competitive recruitment system as defined earlier, but by definition, it is the "best person" who will provide the best quality of service to the public. It is therefore of critical importance that the public service be able to attract a fair share of the best talent in the labour market. The exceptions that follow implicitly assert that recruiting the "best" may not always be the highest priority of the government. This assertion requires a case-by-case justification.

No administration operates a pure merit system . . .

- *Elected officials.* First and obviously, some officials are elected, not appointed.

- *Political appointments.* Those elected officials may hand pick some political advisers. There may be relatively many of them, as in the United States, or relatively few, as in the United Kingdom, but in most cases, they should be narrowly confined to senior staff who are working directly for politicians, thus posing a challenge to administrations where there are many political cadre posts. It also needs to be borne in mind that some civil service systems with a large number of political appointees, such as in France and the United States, may be very merit-oriented because of the selective and competitive nature of the recruitment process.

- *Affirmative action.* Several administrations, including those of Malaysia, Northern Ireland and the United States, have used "quotas" and the like in public appointments to speed up the advance of members of a disadvantaged group such as women, or certain ethnic groups, such as the indigenous majority in Malaysia or the Catholic minority in Northern Ireland. A closely specified quota system can have democratic legitimacy, but alternatives that preserve merit are possible.

- *Internal appointments and transfers; local managers' discretion.* Most administrations have restricted certain promotion posts to existing staff in order to minimize transaction costs and to provide career development opportunities. In the same way, local managers may have discretion to make some appointments.

- *Other appointments.* Succession plans, secondments, reallocation of duties, subcontracting to employment agencies, etc. are other ways in which administrations customarily fill some individual jobs.

. . . and in some cases
merit may even be
overridden

It is probably reasonable that merit should be overridden in some such cases: it would be perverse, for instance, to abolish in the name of fairness a transfer system that was introduced to minimize corruption. However, with the obvious exception of elected officials, there should still be a commensurate procedure that preserves merit as far as possible. This should preferably represent a minimal adaptation of the normal procedure so that transparency is preserved to the extent possible. However, the above-mentioned factors are often in tension with the merit principle, requiring difficult judgements in particular cases.

There are also circumstances in which merit is flouted rather than overridden and where the simple need is to bolster it. One is financial corruption, but there are also other obstacles, such as political patronage (clientelism) and nepotism; various forms of discrimination; faulty definition of the "merit principle"; and politicization of the public service.

Ingraining the merit principle

Culture is able to
perform some of the
functions of structure

Where the merit principle is ingrained and policed by professional peer pressure, the role of institutional arrangements can be downplayed (in modern management-speak, culture is performing some of the functions of structure). Thus, in the United Kingdom, the central recruitment function has actually been privatized and all operational functions have been devolved to line departments. The case for other countries to go at least some distance down the same road has been forcefully argued[16] although once again, a decentralized structure is not always appropriate, as discussed earlier in this chapter. However, other institutional arrangements should also be considered, such as:

- Establishing a central staffing agency (discussed above in the context of the legal framework);

- Legal provisions (hence, for instance, Poland's perseverance with the drafting of a civil service law through several changes of government);

- Separation of the political and administrative spheres;

- Setting up an "elite" senior service (as in Argentina); and

- Drawing up an internal code of conduct.

The arrangements suggested here above will not abolish patronage overnight; indeed, they are constantly threatened by the very pressures that they seek to contain. However, the evidence of countries such as Singapore is that their persistence at least establishes a zone that can be used as a base for extending the influence of merit.

How to identify merit

Merit is not self-
evident, however . . .

Both macro- and micro-issues are important in selection: there is little point in having elaborate institutional arrangements if the content of the selection process is unimproved. Merit is not self-evident, and justice must be seen to be done. Administrations often give effect to these truisms through a system of university-style competitive examination, as in Pakistan and the Republic of Korea, or by scrutinizing educational qualifications, as in Singapore. Such methods are fair and command public confidence. However, they do not recognize merit because the link between what is tested and the requirements of work is weak (one meta-analysis found only a very weak statistical relationship between qualifications and job performance).

On the other hand, sophisticated commercial selection tests widely used in Western countries are not available for sale in most developing countries and transition economies, and recreating them would require a critical mass of organizational psychologists, which very few developing countries possess. Moreover, such methods would not be justified for the bulk of public appointments, including manual appointments (manual and senior professional jobs are equally important in this context). Fortunately, other methods, both valid and practicable, are available: good practice is not the preserve of the wealthy.

> ... commercial selection tests are prohibitively expensive for some governments

In the light of research and organizational practice, a good appointment procedure will have these eight elements (it should be noted that the list includes competence development, a second example of how this activity is pivotal in HRM):

- *A job analysis* leading to a written statement of the duties of the job (the job description) and the competences that the jobholder will need (the competency framework or person specification);

- *An advertisement disseminated to eligible groups,* including a summary of the job description;

- *A standard application form;*

- *A scoring scheme* based on the person specification;

- *A short-listing procedure* to reduce applications, if necessary, to a manageable number;

- *A final selection procedure* based, again, on the person specification and including a panel interview;

- *An appointment procedure* based on the scoring scheme; and

- *Notification of results* to both successful and unsuccessful candidates.

An "assessment centre" procedure, comprising a number of selection methods that include an interview and written or oral activities, as appropriate, remains the gold standard of public selection. It is used in several countries that have borrowed from the United Kingdom model. Recent research shows, however, that the validity of the maligned panel interview can match that of the assessment centre, provided that it is structured, based on job analysis, conducted by trained interviewers and culminates in an appointment that reflects panel members' independent scores. However, using at least a second method at the final stage gives a different, and sometimes corrective, view of the candidate.

> The value of a panel interview can match that of an assessment centre

Merit practices are by no means universal even in industrialized country governments. Moreover, appointments are not made in an organizational vacuum and are affected by the general climate and practices that surround them. This said, strengthening appointment on merit is one of the simplest, most powerful ways in which governments can improve their effectiveness, as repeated throughout the present report.

> Appointment on merit is one of the most powerful ways to improve effectiveness

Developing a pay policy: *attracting and retaining talent*

When government compensation falls, both in absolute terms and relative to alternative remunerative activities, civil servants adjust to the new situation.[17]

Changing demographics and other labour market factors, such as growing competition for talent from the private and non-governmental sectors, are increasingly making the recruitment and retention of quality staff a critical issue in the public sector. Adequate pay is widely considered a key component in improving and sustaining the motivation, performance and integrity of public servants.[18] Conversely, low salary levels result in absenteeism, alternative

> The recruitment and retention of talent in the public sector is increasingly critical

and additional employment, corruption and low productivity. Thus, the development of a pay policy is an integral part of strategic HRM in the public service.

Adequate pay is
a key component
in motivation,
performance
and integrity

Yet, beset by budgetary constraints and embroiled in negotiations with unions on the one side and with donors on the other, it is easy for governments to forget what pay is for. The goal of a pay policy should be to pay public servants enough to attract and retain competent people. Sustaining performance and motivation of public servants should also be an important consideration in the development of a pay policy. For example, wages above the equilibrium level and where sufficient labour market flexibility is guaranteed are likely to increase the opportunity cost to staff of reducing productivity. Higher wages can therefore promote performance-orientation of the civil service.

Botswana is one example of a country that used pay as a key lever to attract and retain quality staff in the public sector. The Presidential Commission on the Review of the Incomes Policy in 1990 was crucial in this respect. The Government allowed market forces to determine pay rates and also acted to "decompress" salaries so that the ratio between the highest and lowest paid civil servants widened substantially between the 1980s and 2002. Its pay rates are now among the highest in sub-Saharan Africa.[19]

That Botswana was able to undertake substantial pay reform in the public service is undoubtedly owing in some part to the country's endowment of natural resources—in this case, diamonds. Yet Botswana is not the only developing country blessed with a substantial endowment of valuable natural resources. A number of other developing countries have similar natural resource endowments but have not been able to improve the conditions of service for public employees. What seems to have made the difference is the strategic and effective management by public institutions of the revenue generated as well as genuine leadership commitment to reform.

Although developing a pay policy is inevitably political and delicate, governments and international donors often succumb to a particular naivety. It is to suppose that governments can achieve anything that they want if only they have the determination to do so. Yet political and fiscal constraints dictate that most governments of developing countries cannot deliver a purely rational and ideal pay reform. As discussed in chapter II (box 3), President Soglo of Benin had been a World Bank Regional Director, but he was unable to follow through on his desired pay reform in the face of opposition from public service unions and Members of Parliament, leading ultimately to his defeat in the presidential election in 1996.

It does not follow that governments are obliged to "roll over", giving in to political lobbies such as public service unions. Instead, a government must strike a fine balance between what is ideal and what important stakeholders will countenance and sustain a programme of gradual reform over several years. Every government needs to take political as well as fiscal constraints into account when it comes to salary decisions in the public service. Since the process is always heavily affected by politics and the scarcity of resources, the luxury of an optimal policy does not always exist.

A pay policy does not determine affordability; rather, affordability is a constraint imposed by the budget. Expenditure on wages should not be budgeted without taking other government expenses into consideration. For example, exhausting the budget on wages and salaries to teachers and doctors may leave little room for the procurement of books and medicine. What is important is to achieve the optimal mix of spending in terms of strategic objectives compared to simply setting a target for expenditure on wages alone.

Key elements of a strategic approach

A pay policy should be strategic in the sense of "satisficing" stakeholders, while at the same time thinking ahead. The alternative is to be "reactive", with the government at the mercy of interest groups whose muscle often has little to do with their contribution to meeting government objectives. Thus, a government needs to start with an appropriate strategy given the circumstances. In a political environment, a delicate balancing act must be performed by juggling key priorities and interests of stakeholders as well as equity and motivation when developing a pay policy. A pay strategy will generally involve the following:

- Bringing pay into line with government's overall policy objectives. This includes identifying any groups of staff (e.g., primary school teachers) that are currently under- or overpaid in areas to which the government wants to give priority. This is how pay contributes to achieving government's strategic objectives;

- Determining the basis for pay and, in particular, the appropriate mix of the following primary as well as secondary factors:

  Primary factors: *Secondary factors:*

  - Affordability   - Cost of living
    (i.e., budget constraints)   - Market-based pay
  - Job content, possibly informed by   - Individual performance
    "job evaluation"   - Qualifications

- Establishing an appropriate "compression ratio" between highest and lowest earners; and

- Striking a balance between pay, other benefits (including pensions) and allowances. It is important to recognize that non-monetary remuneration, such as housing, and promises of benefits to be paid in the future, such as pensions, are a current expense; otherwise, civil service pay will be grossly underestimated.

Balancing equity and motivation

Governments are in general obliged to have a political commitment to equitable pay even where market or performance factors may not justify it. Under some circumstances, however, maintaining equitable pay is simply not tenable. First, pegging equitable pay to a "minimum living wage" may seem like the "right" decision, yet in countries with extremely low per capita income, this equals paying a premium for lower-level staff, which comes with the risk of bloating the public service. Second, even with wages level with or lower than market wages, a "bottom-heavy" public service paid equitably may crowd out other vital government spending plans. Thus equitable pay is not plausible without a "rightsized" public service.

Governments are obliged to commit politically to equitable pay

Motivation, on the other hand, includes using pay differentials to give staff an incentive to seek higher-level responsibilities. Civil service systems have traditionally based salary scales on formal qualifications and job content rather than market factors. However, in recent years, particularly with reference to the NPM model, governments have become aware that they need to link salaries to market wages in order to attract and retain the talent necessary to improve and sustain public sector performance. When income inequality among staff is deliberately increased, senior management positions become more attractive than was previously the case. This is achieved through "salary decompression", which means increasing the ratio between the top and bottom salaries. The higher the ratio, the more decompressed the salaries, and vice versa. The assumption when decompressing and at the same time holding expenditure constant is that lower levels of staff are overpaid while the higher echelons are underpaid.

Pay differentials are key to providing incentives for staff to seek higher-level responsibilities

As table 8 shows, some countries opt for a more egalitarian pay structure, whereas others operate with a larger pay differential between the highest and the lowest grades of the

Table 8.
Selected pay-scale compression ratios, 1991–2003

Country	Early	Late	Reference period
Cambodia	..	2	2002
Cape Verde	5	7	1991–2001
Gambia	8	7	1992–2003
Guinea	..	2	2002
Madagascar	3	5	1997–2002
Mali	7	6	1994–2003
Mauritania	2	2	1993–2002
Pakistan	9	10	1994–2002
Peru	..	3	2002
Senegal	5	4	1994–2001
Suriname	6	3	1997–2002
Timor–Leste	4	4	2002–2004
Togo	4	4	1991–1999
Tonga	..	7	1997
Uganda	4	5	1995–1997
United States	6	6	1994–2004
Yemen	..	3	1998

Sources:
UN/DESA, based on
IMF Country Reports,
World Bank reports and
national statistics.

Note:
The compression ratio is
calculated as the ratio
between the mean of
the highest salary grade
and the mean of the
lowest salary grade,
where possible.

civil service. In theory, an egalitarian pay structure is more attractive to the lower echelons of the civil service, whereas pay structures with greater decompression are considered conducive to recruiting and retaining talent that would otherwise possibly switch to the private sector.

Scope of perquisites

Most people would agree that Cambodia, Guinea and Mauritania, where the average salary ratio between the highest and the lowest grade was only two, needed to "decompress". However, governments need to take allowances and in-kind benefits into account as well. For example, Uganda's moderate compression ratio in the mid-1990s changed to 1:100 after non-monetary allowances and benefits were included.[20] This is often the case in varying degrees, especially in developing countries. In Zambia, for instance, Permanent Secretaries earn 50 times as much as

Perquisites play a
substantial role in
developing countries

the lowest-paid people in the civil service when in-kind benefits (housing, cars, telephones, etc.) are taken into account. However, excluding such benefits, the difference was only fivefold.[21]

In many developing countries, allowances and in-kind benefits play a substantial role in remunerating employees in the public sector, which is why getting the right balance between pay and benefits and allowances is so important. An initial step in pay reform is to consider monetizing these benefits in order to curb the abuse of open-ended privileges and entitlements of public officials. In 2002, Nigeria adopted a monetization policy in order to check the spiraling costs of providing benefits in areas such as accommodation, transport, food, utilities, servants, leave, medicine, furniture, vehicles and drivers. The costs of providing these amenities had become so substantial that they left little room for funding of other government priorities, for instance, capital projects. Yet, as recent developments in Nigeria show, monetizing benefits is not a free lunch, at least not in political terms. Even though non-transparent remuneration is inefficient and inequitable, "increasing transparency prematurely is likely to generate uncontrollable and unaffordable pressure for equalization of benefits and across the board pay increases".[22]

Monetizing benefits is not a free lunch

Moreover, where "moonlighting" and corruption prevail, it is likely that senior civil servants will earn more from these sources than their juniors, once again moderating the effect of salary compression. It should be noted that salary decompression is likely to be gender-negative, as senior public servants are disproportionately male. A comprehensive pay reform needs to take all these factors into account and not simply the "headline" salary rates, which, although a starting point, usually give an incomplete picture of actual earnings of senior public servants. It also must be borne in mind that the multiplicity of sources of earnings of senior officials also increases the costs of administering the government payroll system.

In most developed countries, allowances and in-kind benefits play a small or rather limited role in the total remuneration of staff. In the mid-1990s, for example, the base salary of public servants in France and Germany accounted for 70–90 per cent and 75–95 per cent of total remuneration, respectively, and in the Nordic and Anglo-Saxon countries, it accounted for almost 100 per cent of the total.[23]

Perquisites play a small role in developed countries

Although providing incentives for such things as seniority or assignments to unattractive postings has merit, developing extensive additional, customized pay schemes and supplements comes at a price. In Peru, for instance, only 41 per cent of all salary payments were charged to the formal payroll in recent years. The remaining part of the wage bill was covered by over 40 different salary supplements, whether in cash or in kind. As a consequence, employees in the same salary grade and performing more or less the same functions were at risk of receiving very different wages. The net result was that the internal cohesion of salary grades in the civil service in Peru became abnormally distorted, with even the maximum remuneration of the lowest grade higher than the maximum salary recorded for vice-ministers in exceptional cases.[24] In a response to these adverse effects of customized supplements, the Law for the System of Public Employment Remuneration was being adopted in 2005.

Extensive perquisites may undermine the efficiency and equity of the payroll system

Competitiveness of public sector pay

Of equal if not greater importance is the competitiveness of public sector pay vis-à-vis that of the private sector. It is commonly held that pay in the public sector is much lower than pay in the private sector. However, this conclusion may not apply to all grade levels in the public service. For example, while public sector salaries in Latin America and the Caribbean generally tend to be lower than those offered in the private sector, this may not apply to posts requiring a low level of skills. While senior managers in the public sector are often paid substantially less

Public sector pay is not always lower than in the private sector

The more skills a post requires, the larger the pay differential with the private sector

than their counterparts in the private sector (around 25 to 35 per cent, according to one study), parity is not unheard of for unskilled positions.[25] The experiences of Latin American and Caribbean countries also indicate that the more skills a public sector post requires, the larger the pay differential with the private sector.

These findings are not confined to Latin America and the Caribbean. Examples from such diverse places as Guinea, Pakistan and the former Yugoslav Republic of Macedonia illustrate the need to look at both the compression ratio and the pay differentials between the public and private sectors in order to perform a balanced comparison of salaries at all levels. In Yemen, for instance, the compression ratio in the government was only 1:3 in the late 1990s. In the same vein, senior managers in the private sector received salaries that were nine times higher than those of their counterparts in the public sector, while compensation at the support services level in the private sector was three times higher than that in the public sector although this comparison did not include the low wages paid in the informal economy.[26] Under such circumstances, attracting and retaining the best talent become highly unlikely.

"Secondary remuneration" plays an important part in several countries

Sometimes pay differentials between the public and private sectors can even seem absurd when illustrated by examples. In Mozambique in the early 1990s, for instance, pay differentials were so skewed that a janitor employed by an international organization earned a salary that was the equivalent to that of a director in the public sector. By the late 1990s, however, this ratio had improved so that a driver employed in the private sector earned the equivalent of a lecturer's salary at a public university. Nevertheless, if one took into consideration the apparent differences in living standards, payments associated with "moonlighting" and corruption or what has often been referred to as "secondary remuneration" played a significant part in raising total income.[27]

The presence of donors and NGOs sometimes leads to poaching of quality staff

The presence of high-paying donors and international organizations in developing countries and transition economies has also sometimes led to poaching of the relatively limited number of highly skilled staff in the labour market—staff who would otherwise occupy senior positions in the public sector, as experiences in Cambodia and Mozambique demonstrate. In addition, the topped-up salaries of staff in donor-sponsored Programme Implementation Units have often inhibited the "sunset" absorption of those employees into the public sector. In an attempt to address such problems in Bolivia, some multilateral and bilateral donors are financing a salary enhancement scheme in priority ministries.[28]

Pay in some public sectors is more attractive than that in the private sector

Needless to say, there are examples that defy the general assertion of pay differentials in favour of the private sector. In Morocco, a recent study found that monetary compensation in the public sector is 8 per cent higher than in the private sector. However, if all non-monetary allowances are included in this comparison, the total remuneration of civil servants in Morocco would be between 1.5 and 2 times higher than that in the private sector. This, the study concludes, may explain the significant queues for employment in the public sector in Morocco, particularly by skilled workers.[29]

Compensation should both be equitable and motivate staff

In general, one should expect higher remuneration in the private sector than in the public sector because of job security, often-generous pension benefits and a higher shirking rate in the latter. Hence, it should not necessarily be the aim of governments to match compensation in the private sector across the board. Instead, governments should aim to provide compensation that meets at least minimum living standards for employees at lower levels and at the same time provides incentive for senior managers to stay in the public sector by sufficiently decompressing salaries.

Should higher wages be deemed necessary, government will ideally be hoping for economic growth that is respectable enough to finance the increases. However, even if growth is low, there may be some scope for improving tax revenue collection. Setting up autonomous revenue collection authorities seems to have improved revenue collection in several African countries, including Mozambique and South Africa. Uganda offers a dramatic example: after the establishment of the Uganda Revenue Authority, tax revenue increased nearly five times between 1991 and 1996.[30]

The practice of assigning the responsibility for collecting (certain) taxes to autonomous entities, generally known as tax farming, is said to minimize government administration and result in more efficient tax collection.[31] The primary advantage of this system is considered its ability to generate more gross revenue than direct government collection. The problem, however, is that this kind of tax collection tends to become overzealous with resources over-employed since costs borne by taxpayers, for instance, are not taken into account. This in turn would require government expenses on close monitoring, which would have the potential to offset the initial gain.

Alternatively, government may find money from existing budgets. If, for instance, Sri Lanka or Uganda can reach a lasting settlement with insurgents, spending on security can be cut and savings might be redirected to increasing wages. If this is not possible, however, government is thrown back on the structural adjustment-era remedy of cutting some jobs in order to pay more to the people who really matter.

Tax farming has the potential for breeding overzealousness

Employment and wage data

Considering the growing importance of remuneration in motivating and retaining talented staff in the public sector, it is of some concern that most developing countries and transition economies devote relatively meagre efforts to the collection of quality data on employment and wages. For one reason or another, the availability of good data in this area is very limited, making it difficult, if not impossible, to measure the cost and contribution of human resources to the overall performance of the public sector. The present report therefore recommends that governments give more consideration to the development of better systems and methodologies to further improve the collection and analysis of data on wages and employment in the public sector.

Meagre efforts are devoted to the collection of quality data on employment and wages

First, however, governments need to sort out a number of methodological questions integral to the process of collecting and analysing data on public sector employment and wages. This includes deciding on the scope, timeliness and frequency of data collection as well as the definition of key terms. Wage and salary data, for example, often suffer from the exclusion of non-wage remuneration, as discussed earlier in this section. Needless to say, excluding perquisites, such as pensions, accommodation, automobiles, telephones, meals and clothing, the value of which often far exceeds the base pay, undermines the usefulness of data collection in this area.

Better harmonization of methodologies and standards for the collection of data on employment and wages could improve HRM in the public sector

Another issue of some concern in this area is the lack of common standards among countries for the collection of data on employment and wages in the public sector. Such data are very seldom comparable across countries. These challenges are affected by a number of factors. First, states are structured differently, which inevitably has implications for the comparative utility of data on public sector employment and wages. Centralized states, other things being equal, will generally display a greater percentage of expenditure on wages because fewer financial transfers to lower levels of government take place with subsequent payment of wages at this level of government. Data on wages and salaries as a percentage of total central government expenditure illustrate this point (table 9).

The central governments of India and the United States, for example, do not employ schoolteachers, whereas the central governments of Chile and France do. Obviously, this fact will skew the comparison of data of central government employees and wage levels, as

Table 9.
Wages and salaries in federal versus unitary states

Source:
UN/DESA, based on
World Bank, *World
Development Indicators.*

Note:
Wages and salaries
are displayed as a
percentage of total central
government expenditure.

Country	State	Percentage	Year
United States	Federal	8.4	1997
France	Unitary	15.9	1997
India	Federal	9.4	2001
Chile	Unitary	19.4	2001

does the recording of transfers to lower levels of government as an important component of central government expenditure in federal states. Second, even when states are structured along the same lines, divergent approaches to the classification of public sector employment often pose another daunting challenge for cross-country comparison. This problem is sometimes further aggravated by the frequent reclassification of sectors as a result of administrative reform. Recent developments in service delivery, such as outsourcing, have further skewed the picture when comparing data on employment and wages in the public sector in different countries.

*Strategic HRM
requires quality
data on employment
and wages*

In conclusion, the availability of accurate, reliable, valid and comprehensive data on employment and wages in the public sector is becoming more and more important for the strategic management of human resources. Therefore, it is recommended that governments consider developing better methodologies for collecting and analysing data on employment and wages in the public sector at both the national and global levels.

Performance management and appraisal: *supporting and developing staff*

Appraisal systems are a lot like seat belts. Most people believe that they are necessary, but they don't like to use them.[32]

*Managers should be
responsible for the
performance of staff*

For some governments, such as Morocco, introducing performance management and appraisal is the first step in HRM reform. This is because performance management is a way of telling managers in the public sector something that they may not have heard before: they are responsible for the performance of the staff who work with them, and it is the managers' job to manage them by setting objectives that relate to the overall strategy, monitoring their performance and giving them support, feedback and the opportunity to develop.

The experience of managing performance in developing-country governments shows not only what effective performance management can look like in practice but also how different it is from the traditional practice of many public agencies.[33] At one extreme, the Zambia Electricity Supply Corporation (ZESCO) Ltd., with a new manager committed to improving service quality, had a thorough performance management procedure. In the context of a strategic mission statement with which staff were familiar and of detailed job descriptions for individual posts, objectives were set annually with the participation of individual employees. An annual appraisal meeting lasting at least two hours centred on the supervisor's draft report on the employee's performance. The fact that discussion was often heated showed that it was serious. The emphasis was on improving performance through praise and encouragement and on tackling poor performance, initially through counselling but possibly in the end through dismissal: ZESCO, unlike many public agencies, had effective power to hire and fire.

At the other extreme, in the late 1990s, the Ministry of Health in Guatemala had no formal performance management system whatsoever. Even monthly service delivery reports (e.g., of immunization coverage) and supervision visits to staff in the field often did not take place, partly because of lack of resources. Similarly, up to the mid-1990s, Zambia's only mental health referral hospital relied on an "annual confidential report" system, where reports were written by line managers, typically with no communication with their employees, and forwarded to some central body where they were notionally used for promotion decisions. As a result, there was no sense of a culture of performance in the hospital; on the contrary, staff were often absent from their posts.

It is striking that ZESCO did not link performance management to pay decisions. Establishing a link has its supporters, but it is immensely difficult to make performance-related pay work. Malaysia has possibly gone further than any other developing country, having introduced a system of annual performance-based bonuses in the early 1990s. Early in the new century, however, it decided to step back from it, partially substituting a system of training course-based assessment for the manager's judgement. This was in response to complaints of manager bias made by the civil servants' trade union over a ten-year period, sometimes with an ethnic component.

There is also evidence from the government of at least one industrialized country that performance-related pay can damage performance and motivation rather than improve them.[34] However, in a career public service, there is less difficulty in linking performance management to promotion through mechanisms that many countries have always had even if the link has been tenuous in practice.

As with other HRM practices, there are contextual factors to which governments need to adapt the textbook "good practice" models. One of them is the willingness of politicians to let managers get on with the job and make their own hiring and firing decisions. A second contextual factor is the reaction of public sector trade unions. Attempting to impose a performance management system on staff may be counterproductive. One reason why performance management was moribund in the Zambian teaching hospital was that the Government, faced in 1997 with the threat of a nationwide strike by health service unions, had taken back the power to hire and fire that the 1995 Health Act had given to hospitals. Union opposition to the performance-related pay element of a new scheme proposed in the late 1980s was also the reason why Mauritius still had no effective performance management procedure over ten years later (box 10).

Rightsizing: *getting staffing back on track*

The present report offers a positive agenda for human resource management in the public sector. However, governments must face the fact that from time to time, they will need to reduce spending on staff. Even after recognizing that reducing spending is by no means the same thing as laying off staff, as is explained later on in the report, the need to reduce spending is not always well judged. Governments, such as in the United Republic of Tanzania, have discovered that there may be more scope to reduce government deficits by focusing on improving revenue collection than laying off staff.[35] In this respect, rightsizing resembles other areas of activity where shifts in tactics might be required to achieve results.

Marginal notes:

Performance-related pay may not be the solution

Formal procedures should be in place before introducing performance management

Improved revenue collection is an alternative to firing staff, yet . . .

...contraction is
an inevitable feature
of government

There are three reasons why contraction is probably an inevitable feature of the landscape of government. First, many of the economies from which governments obtain their revenues follow a cycle of "boom" and "bust", veering from growth to stagnation or even recession. Second, governments, especially in poor countries, are affected by external shocks, such as a rise in the cost of oil or a bad harvest. In Morocco, where GDP has tended to track rainfall levels, the late King Hassan once remarked that "faced with a choice between an intelligence report and a weather forecast, I will put the intelligence report on one side".[36] Third, new technology makes it possible to reduce the number of people needed to carry out standardized tasks, such as sending out tax demands. Indian photographer Raghubir Singh's classic 1970s image of Calcutta's Writers' Building, the bureaucratic heart of the West Bengal state government, with its serried ranks of pen-pushers toiling beneath towers of yellowing files, is no longer representative of public administration in either industrialized or developing countries.

A strategic approach to rightsizing

In cases where a government judges that rightsizing would mean reducing the number of staff, how should it go about it? There are three principles to keep in mind. Effective rightsizing will:

- Be strategic, that is, it will start from a strategic view of where government or an individual department is going and a sense of the implications of strategy for staff employment;

- Actually deliver savings, and not merely a crude reduction in the number of employees; and

- Minimize hardship to employees.

Rightsizing is
a form of "turn-
around" management

Despite the impression that rightsizing means an exclusive focus on the "bottom line" (something of which finance ministries and certain donor agencies have occasionally been guilty), this is an area to which the strategic model outlined in this chapter also applies. Something approaching a consensus has developed that "turning around" an organization is a two-stage process where emergency action to stem decline leads to strategic planning for the future: what has been called a "recovery strategy".

Rightsizing is a process that starts with the overall development strategy and HRM plan of the government or the individual department. A management review is conducted within that strategic context and used to generate a re-profiling plan, where appropriate, one that includes measures to minimize hardship to employees, if needed (the phrase "where appropriate" signifies that retrenchment is not a necessary outcome of a review). The voluntary retirement scheme introduced by state-owned banks in India between November 2000 and March 2001 is an example of a successful experience with rightsizing (box 13).

Actual job
reductions should
be the last resort

Concurrently with the rightsizing process, governments need to pay attention to specific process measures since they constitute a continuous concern. These include measures to generate ownership of and commitment to the programme, and consultation and communication with staff and their representatives. The appropriate pace of the programme, which the timetable in the strategy action plan will address, is another process issue. Once the strategic framework is in place, the next step is to try to avoid making job reductions altogether through the following measures:

- *Remove ghosts.* Uganda thought that its initial target for staff reduction of 34,000 jobs was tough until it discovered no fewer than 42,000 ghost workers on its books (i.e., fictitious names included in a payroll, allowing someone falsely to receive a salary);[37]

Box 13

A voluntary retirement scheme—India

The state-owned banks in India were generally considered overstaffed before the implementation of a voluntary retirement scheme (VRS) in 1999. A study undertaken by the Federation of Indian Chambers of Commerce and Industry (FICCI) had revealed that this sector was overstaffed in 1998–1999 by more than 59,000 employees if the benchmark of $233,000 in business per employee (BPE) was used. If the BPE was raised to approximately $291,000, the number shot up to more than 177,000 employees, accounting for 22 per cent of the total staff in 16 nationalized banks. In terms of productivity, BPE and the profit per employee (PPE) of the Indian public sector banks were much lower than the BPE and PPE of comparable private or foreign banks.

Although sometimes criticized for their potentially negative consequences, including lack of financial sustainability, job erosion and brain drain, early retirement schemes are still accepted as an effective human resource development strategy to retrench employees, improve efficiency and productivity, and balance the age and skills composition of the workforce. Between 15 November 2000 and 31 March 2001, the first round of a VRS was implemented in all but one state-owned bank in India. All permanent employees with 15 years of service or who were above 40 years of age or those who had been identified as surplus were eligible to participate in the early retirement scheme. The employees who opted for the retirement plan were entitled to 60 days of compensation for each year of service rendered or the equivalent of the salary for the remaining years of service, whichever was less. Those who were eligible for a VRS but unwilling to opt for early retirement were provided with the option of a five-year sabbatical. To minimize the financial burden created by the VRS, the Government of India allowed the banks to settle the payments in two instalments, with a minimum of 50 per cent of the amount paid in cash immediately and the remaining payment made within six months, either in cash or bonds. The Government encouraged the banks to issue bonds and guaranteed their repayment, including accrued interest.

The overriding goal of the scheme was achieved dramatically in terms of retrenching employees and reducing costs. Out of the total 863,117 employees in the 26 state-owned banks that implemented the initiative, 100,810 (11.7 per cent) staff took the offer, according to a study published in the bulletin of the Indian Banks' Association (IBA). In 2000–2001, the staff cost of all the 27 state-owned banks (including the Corporation Bank, which did not opt for a VRS), was INR 21,050 crore (approximately $4.7 billion). By 2001–2002, it had dropped to INR 18,959 crore (approximately $4.3 billion). Furthermore, the VRS is considered to have helped to balance the skills profile vis-à-vis the employee mix. The next phase of the VRS is expected to focus on the age profile of the workforce.

Encouraged by the initial success of the VRS in its state-owned banks, the Government of India began to introduce a similar scheme in the civil service in September 2004. Senior civil servants, who have between one and five years left before retirement, are eligible to participate in the scheme. They are offered special financial packages consisting of "one-time lump sum" compensation in addition to their regular retirement benefits. It is expected that the new scheme will rationalize the workforce of the civil service and further prepare the Government for the new challenges of ageing, globalization and technology modernization.

Sources:
See Bibliography.

- *Enforce retirement ages.* Uganda discovered several thousand staff still working beyond the official retirement age;
- *Initiate recruitment freezes combined with natural wastage;*
- *Delete empty posts.* These are established posts that have been vacant for some time;
- *Carry out human resource forecasting* in order to anticipate a declining need for staff in some areas or a declining ability to pay for them;

- *Seek "functional flexibility" through "multi-skilling".* In this vein, Ford Motor Company in the United Kingdom, for instance, took action to reduce the number of separate job categories from 516 in 1986 to 45 in 1988;

- *Set up a redeployment procedure* so that staff in a redeployment "pool" must be considered first before a post is advertised in the normal way. It is important to avoid such "pools" being abused as a dumping ground for staff who have fallen from political favour, such as senior civil servants identified with the party previously in power;

- *Organize retraining* to convert, for example, a redundant administrator into a computer programmer; and

- *Anticipate redundancy* by having procedures in place that will enable government to deal with the problem systematically. Such procedures take time to develop, especially where trade unions must be consulted. They should be drawn up as a part of day-to-day HRM practice. In one British local authority, the redundancy agreement drawn up as long ago as 1977 enabled the authority to reduce jobs over a period of several years without making compulsory redundancies.

If, after all that, a government still finds that it needs to reduce jobs, it should consider the following steps, arranged in order of political difficulty:[38]

- *Introduce part-time and flexible working hours;*

- *Appoint new staff on temporary contracts;*

- *End guaranteed entry.* Some governments, such as that of Benin in West Africa, have had a scheme for automatic entry into the civil service for all graduates. Given an increased number of graduates, this is probably no longer appropriate in most countries;

- *Suspend automatic advancement.* Similarly, some countries have had a system of automatic, seniority-based promotion which, apart from its salary implication, weakens the link between promotion and merit;

- *Introduce voluntary redundancy.* This is often welcomed by staff, and quotas can be achieved faster than government might expect (as in the United Kingdom). However, it can be expensive: in Ghana, it consumed two per cent of total government expenditure over the first five years of reform;

- *Privatize/contract out.* This will bring staff numbers down but may not reduce spending: a contracted-out service is not necessarily less costly, as discussed earlier in the report;

- *Freeze salaries;* and

- *Implement compulsory redundancy.*

A striking feature of the above list is that compulsory redundancy, despite the popular image, is only the last item on a long list, and it may never be reached if the government manages to achieve sufficient savings through other means. On the other hand, if redundancies are needed, then any responsible employer will take care to minimize the hardship caused to the staff who are affected (box 14).

Box 14

Rightsizing the right way—Uruguay

Uruguay is a welfare state whose citizens enjoy one of the highest standards of living outside the industrialized world. The country's public sector is faced with numerous challenges, including a disproportionately large civil service. Since the Constitution makes it very hard to dismiss a civil servant, downsizing of the public service had become a very tenuous proposition. Things were further complicated as public employees were often hired based on political connections, which led to the constant creation of new public agencies and divisions, often with little regard for the cost implications. Owing to the oversized public service, the salaries of professionals were also very low, resulting in many qualified employees working only a few hours a day in the public office and spending the rest in a private sector job to supplement their income. According to a government survey in 1995, the people supported public service reform, but only if it would not result in layoffs and social conflict.

The public sector modernization strategy adopted by the Government of Julio Maria Sanguinetti in 1995 followed a two-stage approach that emphasized incentives and voluntary participation instead of job cuts. The Government invited the executing agencies within the central administration to define their core competencies and to identify activities that could be eliminated, transferred to more qualified agencies or even outsourced to private companies. If the restructuring plan was approved by the Executive Committee for the Reform of the State (set up with a $115 million loan from the Inter-American Development Bank), the agency was offered a reward. It was given access to special funds to cover the severance, early retirement or transfer costs of redundant employees. These funds also included technical support, business training and small loans for civil servants who opted to start their own private businesses. Each agency was allowed to keep the savings generated by the restructuring, which could be used to raise the salaries of the remaining staff, invest in training and equipment, and pay performance-based bonuses.

The results of this approach to downsizing were quite spectacular. Out of the 108 executing agencies that participated in the programme, 82 (representing some 80,000 public employees) successfully restructured their operations. A total of 9,221 redundant positions were identified during the restructuring exercise, with more than one third of the staff concerned receiving training and assistance in finding private sector employment. As of 2002, the leaner public service was saving Uruguayan taxpayers $56 million per year; $25 million was going to the national treasury, while the rest was being returned to the restructured agencies to fund the various incentive programmes. The entire downsizing exercise took less than three years to implement and by the end of the process, the number of public agencies had been reduced by 46 per cent. The most remarkable achievement was that during this phase, not a single strike or labour dispute took place. A fundamental factor contributing to the success of the programme was the involvement and full support of the agency chiefs, who saw this exercise as an opportunity to recruit highly qualified staff and to give a pay rise to deserving employees who would otherwise be tempted to join the private sector. The programme also carried political credibility as it was embedded in the national budget, giving the Government adequate time to implement the reforms instead of wasting precious time in political wrangling to generate the required financial resources.

Following the success of the first phase of reform, the Government is embarking on a second phase that will focus on improving the actual performance of the public service. All public agencies, for example, will be required to carefully define their products and services and to come up with specific performance indicators and goals, with public funds in the next budget to be granted on the basis of organizational performance.

Source:
See Bibliography.

Severance payments
can be prudently
administered
by individuals

Retraining schemes at
times render little
practical benefit

Generally speaking, once government has consulted unions and others on its plans, it is probably well advised to concentrate assistance in the size of the lump sum and pension that retrenched employees receive: there is evidence that people make better decisions about how to use such a payment than government will make on their behalf.[39] Advice and information are also important to remove misconceptions and to prepare staff for the change. Retraining schemes to help retrenched employees to acquire new skills are desirable in theory but can be expensive, difficult to administer and poorly targeted so these employees receive little practical benefit.

Notes

1   Council of Europe (2003). Civil Service Reform in Europe. Doc. 9711. Committee on Economic Affairs and Development. Parliamentary Assembly. Available from: http://assembly.coe.int/Documents/WorkingDocs/doc03/EDOC9711.htm

2   World Bank (1997). Checklist on law drafting and regulatory management in Central and Western Europe. Sigma papers: No. 15.

3   Corkery, J. and A. Land (1997). *Civil service reform in the context of structural adjustment: a triangular relationship.* Policy Management Brief No. 7. Maastricht: European Centre for Development Policy Management.

4   McCourt, Willy (2001). Towards a strategic model of employment reform: explaining and remedying experience to date. *International Journal of Human Resource Management,* vol. 12, issue 1, pp. 56–75.

5   Hood, C., C. Scott, O. James, G. Jones and T. Travers (1999). *Regulation inside Government: Waste-Watchers, Quality Police and Sleaze-Busters.* Oxford: Oxford University Press.

6   United Nations (2005). *Innovation and Quality in Government of the 21st Century. Fifth Global Forum on Reinventing Government: Capacity Development Workshops.* Department of Economic and Social Affairs. ST/ESA/PAD/SER.E/84.

7   Government of Canada. In Organisation for Economic Co-operation and Development (2001). Issues and Developments in Public Management: Canada 2001. Available from http://www.oecd.org/dataoecd/39/25/1923850.pdf

8   Johnson, Gerry and Kevan Scholes (2002). *Exploring Corporate Strategy: Text and Cases.* London: Financial Times/Prentice Hall.

9   Taylor, Harry (1992). Public Sector Personnel Management in Three African Countries: Current Problems and Possibilities. *Public Administration and Development,* vol. 12, pp. 193–207.

10   Ulrich, Dave (1998). A new mandate for human resources. *Harvard Business Review,* vol. 76, issue 1 (Jan./Feb.), pp. 124–135.

11   Annan, Kofi, Secretary-General, United Nations. Available from http://www.unodc.org/pdf/iaol/un_competencoies.pdf

12   Centre for Management and Organisation Development (2003). *A Guide to Competency Development in the Civil Service.* Available from http://www.finance.gov.ie/cstc/cstdcresources/cmod_report.pdf

13   Jefferson, Thomas, former President, United States, 1813. In Lester J. Cappon, ed. (1959). *The Adams-Jefferson Letters: The Complete Correspondence between Thomas Jefferson and Abigail and John Adams.* Chapel Hill: University of North Carolina Press. Available from http://press-pubs.uchicago.edu/founders/

14   Rauch, James E. and Peter Evans (2000). Bureaucratic structure and performance in less developed countries. *Journal of Public Economics,* vol. 75, No. 1, (Jan.), pp. 49–71; Peter Evans and James E. Rauch (1999). Bureaucracy and growth: a cross-national analysis of the effects of "Weberian" state structures on economic growth. *American Sociological Review,* vol. 64, No. 5, (Oct.), pp. 748–765; and J. Henderson and others (2003). *Bureaucratic Effects: "Weberian" State Structures and Poverty Reduction.* Working Paper No. 31. Chronic Poverty Research Center. Available from http://www.chronicpoverty.org/cpreports2.htm

15   Anderson, J., G. Reid. and R. Ryterman (2003). Understanding public sector performance in transition countries—an empirical contribution. Washington, D.C.: World Bank. Available from http://www.worldbank.org/wbi/governance/govdonors/pdf/reid.pdf

16 Polidano, Charles and Nick Manning (1996). *Redrawing the lines: service commissions and the delegation of personnel management.* Managing the Public Service: Strategies for Improvement, no. 2. London: Commonwealth Secretariat.

17 Kiragu, Kithinji (2004). Pay reform a critical and complex Public Service issue. Pricewaterhouse Coopers. Available from http://www.pwcglobal.com/gx/eng/about/ind/gov/ifi/pdf/public_service_pay_reform.pdf

18 Kiragu, Kithinji and Rwekaza Mukandala (2003). Public Service Pay Reform (Draft Report). Washington, D.C.: World Bank. Available from http://www1.worldbank.org/publicsector/civilservice/Mayseminar/PayReformStudy.pdf

19 Kiragu, Kithinji and Rwekaza Mukandala (2004). Pay reform and policies report. Development Assistance Committee. Paris: Organisation for Economic Co-operation and Development.

20 Government of Uganda (1994). Management of change: context, vision, objectives, strategy and plan. Kampala: Ministry of Public Service.

21 Keuleers, Patrick (2004). Key issues for consideration when assisting civil service personnel management reforms in developing countries. Subregional Resource Facility for the Pacific, Northeast and Southeast Asia. Bangkok: United Nations Development Programme.

22 Garnett, Harry and Mike Stevens (2000). Establishment Control & Pay Determination. World Bank. Available from http://www1.worldbank.org/publicsector/civilservice/establishment.htm

23 Organisation for Economic Co-operation and Development (1995). In Barbara Nunberg (2000). *Ready for Europe: Public Administration Reform and European Union Accession in Central and Eastern Europe.* World Bank Technical Paper No. 466. Washington, D.C.: World Bank.

24 World Bank (2002). Peru—Restoring fiscal discipline for poverty reduction. Public Expenditure Review. Washington, D.C.: World Bank.

25 Reid, Gary J. and Graham Scott (1994). *Public Sector Human Resource Management: Experiences in Latin America and the Caribbean and Strategies for Reform.* Washington, D.C.: World Bank.

26 World Bank (2000). Republic of Yemen: comprehensive development review, Phase I. Washington, D.C.: World Bank.

27 Sulemane, José A. and Steve Kayizzi-Mugerwa (2001). *The Mozambican civil service: incentives, reforms and performance.* Discussion Paper No. 25. Gabinete de Estudos, Ministério do Plano e Finanças, República de Moçambique. Available from http://www.wider.unu.edu/publications/dps/dp2001-85-dp25.pdf

28 World Bank (2003). Cambodia: enhancing service delivery through improved resource allocation and institutional reform. Integrated Fiduciary Assessment and Public Expenditure Review. Washington, D.C.: World Bank.

29 Agenor, Pierre-Richard and Karim El Aynaoui (2003). Labor market policies and unemployment in Morocco: A quantitative analysis. Washington, D.C.: World Bank.

30 Kiragu, Kithinji and Rwekaza Mukandala (2004). Pay reform and policies report. Development Assistance Committee. Paris: Organisation for Economic Co-operation and Development.

31 Stella, Peter (1992). Tax Farming—A Radical Solution for Developing Country Tax Problems? Working Paper No. 92/70. International Monetary Fund: Washington, D.C.

32 Latham, Gary and Ken Wexley (1993). *Increasing Productivity through Performance Appraisal.* New York: Addison-Wesley.

33 Martinez, Javier and Tim Martineau (2000). Measuring and monitoring staff performance in reforming health systems. Research Project PN10. Available from http://www.liv.ac.uk/lstm/hsr/hsrpn10.html

34 Marsden, David and Ray Richardson. (1994). Performing for pay? The effects of "merit pay" on motivation in a public service. *British Journal of Industrial Relations,* vol. 32, issue 2, pp. 243–261.

35 Dia, Mamadou (1996). *Africa's Management in the 1990s and Beyond: Reconciling Indigenous and Transplanted Institutions.* Washington, D.C.: World Bank.

36 Quoted in C. R. Pennell (2000). *Morocco since 1830: A History.* London: Hurst Pennell, p. 324.

37 Government of Uganda (1994). Op cit.

38 See McCourt, Willy (2001). Towards a strategic model of employment reform: explaining and remedying experience to date. *International Journal of Human Resource Management,* vol. 12, issue 1, pp. 56-75; and Barbara Nunberg (1994). Experience with civil service pay and employment reform: an overview. In *Rehabilitating Government: Pay and Employment Reform in Africa,* David L. Lindauer and Barbara Nunberg, eds. Washington D.C.: World Bank, pp. 119–159.

39   Younger, Stephen (1996). Labour market consequences of retrenchment for civil servants in Ghana. In *Economic Reform and the Poor in Africa,* David E. Sahn, ed. Oxford: Clarendon Press, pp. 185–202.

Chapter VI
Promoting organizational learning in the public service

Many observers believe that governments lack the ability to learn and adapt to circumstances of rapid change. Governments tend to experience great difficulties in diagnosing problems early, selecting policy directions, designing effective and efficient programmes, rectifying problems and avoiding what is commonly referred to as "public sector failure". As a result of these capacity gaps, some countries have not been able to take advantage of the many opportunities offered by rapid advances in the economic and technological spheres. An important quality of organizations capable of learning, on the other hand, is their adeptness in identifying and analysing salient cues in the broader environment as well as responding to those cues in an effective and timely manner.

Enabling early response to salient cues is a key feature of organizational learning

Governments and the people of whom they are composed have always been faced with uncertain times and complex choices, but the speed, scale and scope of ongoing changes are exceptional in world history. These challenges place new and often highly complex demands on the capacity of governments to analyse emerging issues and to respond to them effectively. Most governments are therefore in great need of revitalizing their analytical and policy-making capacities, particularly at the central level. An important purpose of such systems is to detect problems facing the government and society as a whole and to propose solutions to address them. In short, governments need to build a culture of organizational learning that will foster continuous reinvention of the public service.

The public service must build the capacity to reinvent itself

There is, however, the general perception that the analytical and technical capacities of governments in many developing countries have been allowed to erode over time for various reasons. These include:

The analytical capacities in developing countries have eroded in recent years

- Growing politicization in the public service;

- Weakening of the ability of the executive to recruit and retain high-quality talent;

- Decline in the importance of policy analysis units vis-à-vis political advisers, particularly in line ministries;

- Lack of statistics collection and analysis; and

- Greater emphasis on the management role of senior government officials vis-à-vis their policy-making role, often as the result of NPM.

As highlighted in chapter II, the quality of institutions in the public sector is underpinned by the capacity of human resources and leadership. Considering that public institutions exist to coordinate action and behaviour for the public interest, it is important to ensure that human resource capacities are properly aligned with the strategic objectives of government. The development of staff competencies is an essential part of a strategy to upgrade these capacities and consequently the quality of the public service. Competence-based staff development, discussed in the previous chapter, also allows for the identification of "performance gaps" of public servants that can then be addressed through capacity-building and organizational learning programmes.

Organizational culture: *changing mindsets*

It has long been established that the quality of the organizational culture matters greatly for institutional performance. Yet with culture shaped by many factors, including social values and norms, the leadership qualities of senior public officials and more generally the HRM polices that have been put in place in the public service, the answers as to how to improve the quality of the organizational culture are numerous.

The quality of organizational culture matters for performance

Compliance: *a virtue turned vice*

A predominant characteristic of a traditional public service is authority vested in hierarchy. Originally, this form of public administration was intended to ensure clear accountability of staff for the completion of tasks, as discussed in chapter I. However, the downside of strict adherence to hierarchical authority is that it tends to evoke compliance in government bureaucracies rather than commitment to the work at hand. The more strongly hierarchical power is exerted, the more results are generally focused on compliance. Yet the genuine commitment of staff is usually an essential factor in fostering meaningful change in any organization.

Bureaucracies tend to evoke compliance rather than commitment

A compliance culture also tends to stifle staff initiative and communications—both critical attributes of organizational learning and performance improvements. If staff are expected only to comply with rules and regulations, little or no incentive will exist for "thinking out of the box" or taking action when it comes to improvements to organizational processes or products. This represents a one-dimensional perception of accountability and a highly negative view of experimentation and mistakes. Traditionally, the virtue of a public servant has been the rigorous pursuit of assigned tasks according to the systems and procedures in place. However, the "assigned tasks" must be the right ones and the "systems and procedures" in place must be flexible enough to accommodate change. In many bureaucracies, on the other hand, these conditions may not be in place, and the rigorous pursuit of the "assigned tasks" has turned into a vice.

Virtue has turned into vice

An organizational culture dominated by rigid adherence to rules and regulations very seldom encourages staff to ask challenging questions and to alter the status quo. In many public services, in fact, the practice of questioning the status quo is not in accord with conventions, and in some instances, the practice is even actively discouraged. Therefore, the challenge for many reform-minded governments is often to radically change the mindsets of both leaders and public servants in order to allow for new forms of communication, initiative-taking and learning to emerge in the public service. A bureaucracy that operates in a traditional and hierarchical way is not well suited to achieve this goal. When leaders in the public sector become conscious of these constraints of traditional public administration, an important step towards enhanced organizational learning has already taken place.

Mindsets structure practices and procedures

Organizational learning: *a people-centred framework*

The difference between traditional approaches to public sector reform and the concept of organizational learning is that the former is typically anchored in top-down technical blueprints while the latter is rooted in a belief that the solution to all problems facing the public service lies in the transformation of the public servants themselves. In a sense, organizational learning provides a bottom-up, people-centred framework to unlock the human potential in

Organizational learning provides a bottom-up and people-centred framework the public sector. The two approaches are therefore based on two very different outlooks on how to reform the management of the public sector.

Generally, improved public sector performance means the provision of better services, the development of more thoughtful policy analysis or the achievement of greater efficiency in public administration. An important cultural attribute of an institution promoting organizational learning is that it tries to strive for an optimum balance between action, dialogue and reflection in the organizational culture. These organizational competencies complement each other. To achieve this balance, it is important that governments undertake regular reviews and evaluations of their work to ensure that problems are identified early and remedial action is taken.

The concept of organizational learning acknowledges that public management in today's complex environment is not a mechanical dispensation of tasks that can be programmed well into the future, but rather requires the constant development of new staff competencies and skills if the public is to be well served. The bureaucratic model as a form of public administration has not proved to be well suited to foster such dynamic adaptation of staff competencies in the public sector. This is one of the reasons why the report advocates for a new synthesis of the best attributes of traditional public administration, public management and responsive governance. Traditional public administration, for example, can greatly benefit from selective infusion of principles and practices from the public management and responsive governance models, as discussed in the previous chapter. The responsive governance model, in particular, places much more emphasis on the potential of the organizational learning concept to reform public administration by stressing the participation of all stakeholders in the process.

Recognition of the professionalism and knowledge of staff is central to the development of organizational learning in the public service. In traditional bureaucracies, the prestige and remuneration of staff are determined primarily by rank rather than degree of professionalism or knowledge. This means that staff aspiring to senior positions are often generalist managers rather than knowledge leaders. On the other hand, organizations whose livelihood depends on knowledge-generation and dissemination, such as universities, think tanks and consulting firms, generally place much greater emphasis on the development of mechanisms that recognize and reward innovation, professionalism, productivity and knowledge leadership of staff.

In many ways, the operational environment in the public sector is becoming more similar to that of the private sector. Public institutions are therefore under growing pressure to act like knowledge- and expert-based organizations. This will have implications for both staff development and HRM in the public sector. Governments can greatly facilitate organizational learning in the public sector by developing an enabling environment that encourages staff to acquire, share and manage knowledge, to network and collaborate with colleagues and external partners, to document lessons learned and other tacit knowledge, to constantly look to the future, and to build up their skills in accordance with a competence-based capacity development framework, such as the one discussed in the previous chapter.

The application of a strategic approach to HRM in the public sector is particularly aimed at creating an adaptive, flexible workforce that has the appropriate incentives to produce, acquire, process and share knowledge. This requires that every level of government be taken into consideration when planning, implementing and executing learning initiatives. A government committed to organizational learning would therefore do well to invest in the development of highly professional HRM capacities.

If the whole idea of the promotion of organizational learning in the public service is to encourage public servants to learn more efficiently and effectively from their own experiences in order to improve the quality of public management, it becomes very important for

Action, dialogue and reflection need to be appropriately balanced

Planning for the future means managing today

Staff must be recognized for professionalism and knowledge

The operational environments of the public and private sector are converging

Professional HRM is a prerequisite for organizational learning

governments to put in place an enabling environment that provides the right incentives for staff to do so. Critical to the organizational change process is the ability of staff, both individually and collectively, to learn from their own experiences, both successes and failures. This collective wisdom and knowledge of staff enable the public service to move from its inherited condition to the target destination.

Governments have many ways to promote organizational learning in the public service. On one hand, they can focus on strategies that encourage greater sharing of both explicit and tacit knowledge among staff, and, on the other, they can emphasize incentives for public servants to take more direct charge of their own capacity-building needs within an overall corporate HRM strategy. The report will focus on four potential areas to facilitate organizational learning and performance improvements in the public service:

- Improve knowledge-sharing and management;
- Promote mentoring programmes for staff;
- Enhance the analytical capacity of government; and
- Strengthen the career development system.

The first three areas emphasize the need to develop mechanisms that facilitate the exchange and creation of both explicit and tacit knowledge among staff, while effective career development promotes individual excellence by creating incentives for public servants to acquire new skills and competencies. Mentoring facilitates the transfer of tacit knowledge from senior staff to younger colleagues in the organization. Analytical capacities are needed to evaluate past experiences and to develop forward-looking scenarios, in short, to create knowledge that can be used to improve the performance of the government. A well-managed career development system promotes greater performance-orientation among staff, which is integral to the organizational learning concept. At the individual level, an effective career system enables staff to move from their current level of competencies towards greater professional development and growth.

Strategic areas to promote organizational learning

Improve knowledge-sharing and management

Fostering trust, dialogue and networking is essential in unlocking the human potential in organizations

An important objective of the organizational learning process is to promote trust, dialogue and networking among staff that can foster the formation of social capital and thereby contribute to more dynamic communications, knowledge-sharing and management in the public service. Such communication processes can either be facilitated or hindered by the existing institutional structures in the public sector. In traditional bureaucracies, for example, institutional structures and cultural characteristics are often not conducive to effective communications and knowledge-sharing among staff, as mentioned earlier. Progressive and reform-minded organizations, on the other hand, use technology and incentives in addition to normal person-to-person exchange to encourage staff to share knowledge and to collaborate.

Well-established networks save time and resources

Effective networking and teamwork may not only facilitate the timely completion of tasks but also improve the quality of work. For instance, in cases when a long time may be spent in trying to solve a particular problem, effective networking, collaboration and knowledge-sharing with peers may reduce this time considerably and thereby contribute to organizational learning. The most productive staff members in any organization are generally those with a very strong ability to network and collaborate with both internal colleagues and external partners. The promotion of a culture of networking, knowledge-sharing and collaboration is therefore an essential part of the organizational learning process in the public service.

The Government of South Africa has actively targeted the need to foster greater knowledge-sharing in the public service by launching the Learning & Knowledge Management Unit in 2001. The Unit is expected to improve horizontal collaboration and networking across ministries or, as one senior manager in the public service expressed it, "People from the Health sector need to understand how their colleagues in Education, Safety, Justice, Social Development, and so on work and which challenges they face in their respective sectors".[1] By means of learning networks, annual conferences and other initiatives, the programme facilitates the sharing of good practices among the staff of government agencies in order to enhance organizational performance in the South African public sector.

Governments also increasingly realize that the ICT revolution offers new ways to unlock the human potential in the public sector by offering user-friendly ways for staff to create, share and apply knowledge in their daily work. How organizations integrate knowledge-sharing strategies, such as "communities of practice", on-site training sessions, daily or weekly debriefings, peer feedback, and formal mentoring and coaching, into institution-building can significantly impact their overall performance. The design of such communication processes is therefore of great importance for organizational learning, as the usefulness of learning strategies will ultimately be judged by their positive impact on the institutional performance.

However, there are significant hurdles to jump over in for public organizations attempting, particularly in developing countries, to create an effective knowledge management system. First, staff often have little incentive—financial or otherwise—to share knowledge with other colleagues. One way to address this is to try to make knowledge-sharing an integral part of performance assessment of staff. Another option is to recognize publicly the staff most active in knowledge-sharing in the organization. Second, it is very difficult to capture the tacit knowledge of staff. Doing so will require organizations to either encourage the more experienced staff to mentor and coach the younger professionals or provide adequate opportunities for senior public servants to document and codify their tacit knowledge. Third, resistance to change should not be underestimated in any organization attempting to introduce knowledge management practices. Many staff may be uncomfortable with sharing their knowledge with other colleagues. Overcoming such resistance will require education and coaching of the staff concerned. Fourth, more openness and knowledge-sharing raise the question of how to create appropriate protocols to handle sensitive and confidential information. All these issues need to be addressed in the development of a knowledge management strategy in the public service.

Promote mentoring programmes for staff

Organizational learning can be further facilitated in certain environments by fostering a culture of mentoring among staff. Mentoring usually involves offering guidance and advice, particularly when an experienced person imparts knowledge, skills, values and attitudes to a more junior colleague in order to facilitate professional and career development. Mentoring relationships are undoubtedly an untapped resource in the public service in many countries and the development of such relationships needs to be facilitated.

The use of mentoring as an instrument for organizational learning is by no means a new concept, however. In some societies, the idea of mentoring is an integral part of the

Horizontal collaboration and networking across ministries represent one important aim of organizational learning

ICTs offer user-friendly ways to create, share and apply knowledge

Staff often have little incentive to share knowledge

Resistance to change is a key obstacle

Mentoring is an untapped resource in the public service

national culture. In Japan, for instance, it is common practice, where the *sempai* (senior)-*kohai* (junior) relationship is an institution in itself not only in the public service but throughout society. In other countries, the notion of a mentoring relationship between a senior and a junior person is not so widespread in society in general, yet it is still well established in both the private and public sectors. It is also very common in universities, where professors become mentors to their students.

Formalized mentoring usually serves the following purposes through different programmes and schemes within the public service:

- Helping new staff to settle in and "'learn the ropes";
- Attracting, retaining and developing talented staff; and
- Contributing to career development for potential managers.

In Japan and Singapore, the practice of assigning a mentor to new entrants is a common practice. More recently, the Government of Slovenia has adopted explicit provisions for the role of mentoring in career development in the public service. It provides that people entering state bodies and local administrations for the first time undergo a preparation period while studying for the relevant professional examination. The preparation periods are ten months for the "'state public administration examination", eight months for the "expert administrative examination" and four to eight months for the "expert examination for the independent execution of accompanying tasks". A mentor, appointed by a principal, determines the individual capacity-development needs and is furthermore responsible for the training itself. In order to provide appropriate incentives during the training, the preparation period may be reduced by up to one third on the proposal of the mentor.[2]

Mentoring can also be used to attract, retain and develop talented staff. In 2001, the former Department of Labour and Administration in Norway initiated the first-ever cross-departmental trainee programme in eight departments. The purpose was to recruit and retain talented young graduates. The participants, recruited both internally and externally and not older than 35 years of age, followed the programme for 14 months. Internal candidates were not allowed to have more than four years of service. During these 14 months, they were exposed to work in three different departments, with supervision and mentoring provided by senior staff. In addition to the work in the departments, six thematic gatherings were held to facilitate knowledge-sharing and learning. In early 2003, 9 out of the 10 first participants worked in one government department or another and the decision was taken to initiate the programme again in the fall of 2003.[3]

Fast-track programmes put candidates on a path to senior management

Providing career development through mentoring has also proven effective over time. Several countries (e.g., Singapore and the United Kingdom) have opted for fast-track programmes where high-flying candidates are put on a path to senior management under the guidance and advice of mentors. Sometimes mentoring by targeting the career development of a particular group within the public service is able to serve several purposes. In Norway, for instance, mentoring has been used to both prepare and promote women at mid-level for senior management positions, thus enhancing female representation in the upper echelons of government.[4] Here, mentoring becomes a joint instrument for capacity development and diversity management. A similar approach has also been attempted in the United Kingdom with the pilot "Elevator Partnerships", where 53 junior women were paired with senior women for one year. At least 18 of the junior women have since been promoted, and at least another seven have moved horizontally (see also chapter III).[5]

Regardless of the individual practices that a public service chooses, it is crucial that a mentorship programme be underpinned by a clear vision and strategy. In other words, the different steps associated with implementing a mentorship programme should be aligned with the overall HRM strategy in the public service. Furthermore, it is important that a mentorship programme be congruent with the desirable values of the organization; it must be tied to the culture. An important objective of a mentorship programme is always to further enhance the performance of the organization. However, as mentioned in the previous section, it is not only excellence that people emulate. Considering that a relationship between a mentor and a protégé is often more tightly knit than that between a leader and staff, the importance of a mentor acting as a role model becomes even more critical.

Mentorship programmes need to be congruent with desirable values . . .

. . . and be tethered to an enabling culture

Enhance the analytical capacity of government

As mentioned at the outset of this chapter, to stay relevant and effective, the public service must develop capacity to reflect deeply about complex issues and anticipate major emerging challenges. This generally includes developing strong capacities for policy-making and analysis. It also means that core government organs, such as finance and planning ministries and other institutions charged with inter-ministerial and horizontal responsibilities as well as selected policy think tanks need to evolve highly effective capabilities for reflection, analysis and evaluation of important policy issues. Building such capacities at the centre of government is usually a very cost-effective investment that can offer great development benefits for the respective country.

The ability of governments to attract and retain talent in the public service is critical for improvements in analytical policy-making capacities since people constitute the "brain power" of government. In improving such systems, it is particularly important to invest in the development of highly qualified policy professionals—the intellectual backbone of the public service. Their ability to prepare options, analysis, forward-looking scenarios and recommendations for decision-making is central to the effectiveness of the policy-making system as well as to organizational learning in general. For example, authoritative statements by a respected policy department often carry enormous weight in shaping the opinions of public servants and policy-makers in most countries. Great care should therefore be devoted to the formation of this group of policy-makers to ensure that they are not only trained in the relevant technical disciplines but also well acquainted with the administrative traditions and culture of the country.

Strengthen the career development system

Governments often incur high opportunity cost because the motivation and energy of staff in the public service are undermined by ineffective career development policies. Lack of career development opportunities arguably constitutes one of the primary factors affecting the ability of the public service to retain high-quality staff. As a result, staff become frustrated and the best talent is inclined to leave for greener pastures in the private or non-governmental sectors. In such cases, the cost to governments in terms of lost tacit knowledge and institutional memory can be quite significant, not to mention the often high cost of replacing staff.

Lack of institutionalized career development affects retention rates

Thus, the formulation of effective career development policies is important for two main reasons. First, the availability of rewarding careers is closely correlated with the performance of public organizations (see chapter II) and thereby organizational learning. Career management of staff is also emerging as a crucial HRM issue in traditional public administration

Career management of staff is emerging as a crucial HRM issue systems in both developed and developing countries. Second, the ability of governments to retain high-caliber staff is essential for the maintenance of institutional memory and the organizational knowledge base. Excellence in recruitment, induction and training will be of little use in such organizations if the staff to whom all these resources have been devoted leave earlier than expected. All organizations need a degree of stability and continuity to perform effectively in the long run. In many surveys, the need of staff for rewarding career development opportunities has been ranked as one of the factors most affecting job satisfaction and staff retention in the public sector.

Learning by doing, exemplified by initiatives such as on-the-job training, job rotation and special assignments, is often considered one of the most important and effective strategies for career development. In Canada, the Public Service Human Resources Management Agency of Canada is responsible for a number of career development programmes. One of these initiatives is the Career Assignment Programme (CAP), originally adopted in 1968 and redesigned in 1998. The target group of the programme in the beginning was senior executives, but it was later broadened to include those considered as having senior management potential.

CAP, which is a management development programme intended for the federal public service, targets a representative group of public servants with the aim of accelerating their professional development and advancement in the civil service. The purpose of CAP is to equip participants with the necessary competencies and skills to assume senior management positions in the public service. The learning component consists of both educational courses and assignments in selected public organizations. The assignments, called "stretch assignments", provide the participants with learning opportunities in functions or areas beyond their past experiences and current level of competency. Assignment agreements are used to formalize this process. The duration of the CAP programme is usually between one and four years, and it is expected that each assignment will last approximately one year. Of those who graduate from the programme, 80 per cent are appointed to senior management positions within one year.

Learning by doing is one of the most effective strategies for staff development

Leadership as the facilitator of learning

The process of transforming the public sector in many developing countries will require action at every level of government—from leaders themselves, from politicians, from human resource managers and from all those involved in public service delivery. While the concept of leadership may be understood differently in different cultures, it is generally seen as a process, consisting of a series of ongoing interactions between a leader and others. Leadership also involves influence because leaders motivate other people to do things and it takes place in a group context, involving a number of individuals and a common purpose.[6] As a result, leadership skills are emerging as one of the most critical competencies of senior public servants, as discussed earlier in the report.

Building on the conceptual underpinnings of the responsive governance model, discussed in chapter I, it is suggested that leaders can further facilitate organizational learning and reform in the public service by focusing their efforts in three important areas: first, by spearheading participatory development of a vision for public sector reform; second, by motivating and bringing out the best in staff; and third, by encouraging more direct involvement of stakeholders in the implementation of reform and thereby promoting greater responsiveness and accountability of public servants to the needs and concerns of citizens and clients in society.

It is generally acknowledged that an important element in successful leadership of reform is vision. The vision, however, cannot be the product of one person; rather, it needs to be developed in partnership with staff and key stakeholders. A shared vision must build on the individual visions of staff in the organization. This requires that employees have a clear view of the bigger picture both in terms of the challenges facing the organization and where it is heading. Thus, what characterizes a leader is the ability to facilitate the development of a common vision that expresses the aspirations of both staff and key stakeholders with regard to where the organization wants to be in the future. To be effective, the vision needs to be persuasive, attractive and optimistic for all those who are part of the organization. It also must be both challenging and feasible. The development of a shared organizational vision can help to instil a culture of trust, collaboration, equity and democracy.

A vision needs to be persuasive, attractive and optimistic . . .

The development of a shared vision can also become the starting point for organizational change and reform. This point has been well exemplified by the Federal Office for Migration and Refugees (BAMF) in Germany (box 15).

. . . and be formulated through a participatory process

Another key role of a leader spearheading reform is to motivate staff by championing the values, norms and standards of the organization. The role of leadership by example in this respect is critical. The term "leading by example" indicates the transformational power of leadership when employees follow the example of a leader. This will require high-level skills combined with strong commitment and determination on the part of the organizational leadership. Needless to say, leading by example also requires that the actions of the leader be worthy

Leading by example embodies the transformational power of leadership

---

Box 15

Developing a shared vision—Germany

The Federal Office for Migration and Refugees (BAMF) in Germany has recently gone through a change process, where its mission was redefined from that of an asylum authority to a government migration policy centre. Prior to 2002, the work of the Federal Office was limited mainly to dealing with asylum applications, but it has since been expanded to include a more comprehensive set of services relating to migration, integration and return of refugees.

To be able to deliver on the new policy, BAMF had to undertake an internal consultative process to redesign its organizational vision and strategy. An important part of this exercise was to discuss its impact on HRM policies, systems and practices in the organization. The process of developing the vision was guided by the following principles:

- Opportunity for all employees to participate;
- Voluntary participation;
- Transparency and comprehensibility of the process; and
- Support by management and the staff council.

At the outset of the reform process, the main challenge facing the leaders of BAMF was to deal with resistance to change from employees. The process suffered from low participation of staff, and discontent was regularly evidenced through negative comments. However, as a result of the keen intent of the leadership of BAMF to forge a genuinely shared organizational vision, combined with a transparent approach and responsive management of the process, staff eventually began to change their attitudes and actively participate in the exercise.

Moreover, the process of redefining the vision of BAMF enabled the management and staff to discuss and resolve a host of other internal problems, which greatly improved communication between management and employees during the reform process. The strong involvement of both staff and management in this exercise was undoubtedly a key success factor in the transformation of BAMF.

Sources:
See Bibliography.

of imitation, yet it would be naïve to think that people emulate only excellence. People learn from their leader, whether this is intended or not. An open, democratic and proactive leader, for example, is likely to instil similar qualities in the organizational culture.

Action speaks louder than words

This learning process also requires that leaders "walk the talk" and demonstrate through their own actions that they are committed to the reform agenda. Subordinates are generally very observant about the behaviour of their managers, and actions always speak louder than words. This was certainly the case in Namibia, where the Auditor General made special efforts to inculcate a culture of trust and open communication and questioning among staff. By doing so, the Auditor General unwittingly facilitated organizational learning (box 16).

Governance models focus heavily on citizens as stakeholders

Leaders can also accelerate organizational learning and reform in the public service by creating an environment where citizens and stakeholders can be directly involved in the transformation of the public sector. The responsive governance model is particularly relevant in this context. It emphasizes a government that is open and responsive to civil society, more accountable and better regulated by external watchdogs and the law.[7] Governance models thus tend to focus more on incorporating and including citizens in all their stakeholder roles rather than simply satisfying customers. A common theme running through the responsive governance model is the importance of multiple forms of public accountability. It depicts diverse, complex forms of 360-degree accountability in which there are multiple stakeholders in both government and society, all of whom have a claim to be heard and answered.[8] By making public servants more accountable to citizens and stakeholders in society, leaders can foster a more responsive and efficient public service that learns faster and delivers better results for its clients.

Greater accountability of senior officials to citizens and stakeholders can act as a catalyst for organizational learning and reform

Box 16

Leading by example—Namibia

When Namibia gained independence in 1990, the country inherited an administrative structure from the departing South African regime that had operated with Pretoria as its headquarters. From the outset, the Government of Namibia was faced with an urgent need to undertake comprehensive civil service reform. One of the public organizations that went through a major transformation during the first half of the 1990s was the Office of the Auditor General (OAG). Its success was attributed mainly to exceptional leadership exercised by the Auditor General, who, incidentally, was an economist, not an auditor, by training. Because of this educational background, the Auditor General had to rely heavily on his subordinates for professional knowledge, which meant creating a culture of openness, questioning and trust. Owing to his distinctive leadership style, staff were also encouraged to ask questions and seek solutions to problems, a phenomenon not common in most African bureaucracies at the time.

Organizational learning in the OAG was further facilitated by the positive attitude of senior managers, who fully shared the vision of the Auditor General to move towards a more open and participative management style. The managers were also prepared to undertake training in how to foster the development of organizational learning in the public sector. A team of Swedish consultants who were involved in providing on-site training for staff also played a very constructive role in promoting a culture of questioning and learning in the OAG. Furthermore, the training budget of OAG was raised significantly, as its positive impact on performance was increasingly recognized. A remuneration system linked to performance provided additional incentives for staff to become more productive and innovative. All these factors not only enhanced the performance of the OAG but also raised the morale of staff. Widely publicized performance audits of public organizations also raised the prestige of the OAG and helped to reinforce a culture of organizational learning.

Sources:
See Bibliography.

Notes

1   Radebe, Thuli (2003). The public service as a learning organisation, *Service Delivery Review,* vol. 2, no. 3. Available from http://www.dpsa.gov.za/sdr_vol2_no3.asp

2   Civil Servants Act of the Republic of Slovenia (2002); and European Industrial Relations Observatory (2002). New law regulates public employment and labour relations. European Foundation for the Improvement of Living and Working Conditions Available from http://www.eiro.eurofound.eu.int/about/2002/08/feature/si0208104f.html

3   Government of Norway (2001). Trainee-programme for Departments. Press Announcement no. 8. Department of Labour and Administration; and Johnny Gimmestad (2003). Trainees on collision course. *Aftenposten.* 23 February. Available from http://www.aftenposten.no/jobb/article495999.ece

4   Organisation for Economic Co-operation and Development (2002). Norway. Paris: OECD. Available from http://www.oecd.org/dataoecd/53/59/33881226.pdf

5   Government of the United Kingdom. Civil service diversity. United Kingdom Cabinet Office. Available from http://www.diversity-whatworks.gov.uk

6   Bryman, Alan E. (1992). Charisma and Leadership in Organizations. London: Sage; and Ralph M. Stogdill (1950). Leadership, membership and organization, *Psychological Bulletin,* vol. 47, pp. 1–14.

7   World Bank (1994). *Governance: the World Bank's Experience.* Washington, D.C.: World Bank; and David Williams and Tom Young (1994). Governance, the World Bank and liberal theory. *Political Studies,* vol. 42, issue 1, pp. 84–100.

8   Behn, Robert (2001). *Rethinking Democratic Accountability.* Washington, D.C.: Brookings Institution Press.

Technical summary
Public sector performance, prestige and promotion

This technical summary provides a synopsis of quantitative analysis for the present report.[1] The analysis consists entirely of linear multiple regressions applied to cross-country data. The sources of data for the quantitative analysis are surveys of expert opinion from the International Country Risk Guide (between 97 and 140 countries),[2] the State Capacity Survey (between 97 and 129 countries),[3] and a survey first carried out for 35 countries by James E. Rauch and Peter Evans,[4] later extended by the United Nations University[5] to cover an additional 16 African countries. In the quantitative analysis, the data from the surveys conducted by Rauch and Evans and the UNU were consolidated into one dataset. Of the 51 countries, a total of 45 are developing countries. Data from the International Monetary Fund, OECD and the World Bank were also used for this analysis.

Public sector performance

The quantitative analysis looks at the effect of differences in structural variables on outcomes, holding per capita income constant and also controlling for the impact of other structural variables. Selected findings include the following:

Professionalism of civil servants is an excellent predictor of both the quality and the integrity (absence of corruption) of the public service, and its effects are consistently positive (see scatter plots 1 and 2).

Scatter plot 1.
Bureaucratic quality and merit

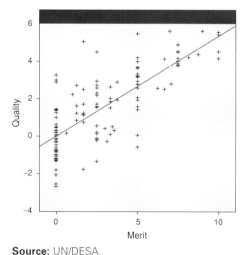

Source: UN/DESA.

Note: Plot of quality against merit in 1999 (121 countries), controlling for selected variables.

Scatter plot 2.
Integrity and merit

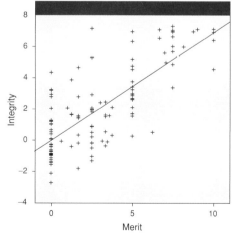

Source: UN/DESA.

Note: Plot of integrity against merit in 1999 (121 countries), controlling for selected variables.

Salaries have some
effect on quality but
a much stronger
impact on integrity

Legal remuneration (salary plus perquisites) of senior public officials relative to counterparts in the private sector has some positive effect on bureaucratic quality and a much stronger positive correlation with integrity (see scatter plots 3 and 4).

Scatter plot 3.
Bureaucratic quality and salary

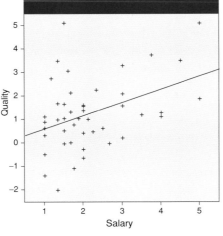

Source: UN/DESA.

Note: Plot of quality against salary in 1990
(45 countries), controlling for selected
variables.

Scatter plot 4.
Integrity and salary

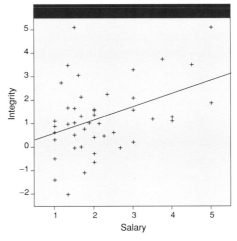

Source: UN/DESA.

Note: Plot of integrity against salary in 1990
(45 countries), controlling for selected
variables.

There is no significant
correlation between
bribes and public
service quality

Extra-legal remuneration (tips and bribes) of public officials is negatively correlated with integrity, but this is true by definition; thus, it is a spurious relationship. More meaningful is the absence of any significant impact of this variable on the quality of bureaucracy in the public sector.

Entrance examinations in the civil service provide only weak evidence for a positive effect on bureaucratic quality. There is also no evidence of any association between examinations and integrity. This unexpected finding may be explained by the fact that the design of the statistical test does not allow for the possibility of relying on university credentials in lieu of examinations to screen applicants.

NPM is not a
significant determinant
of the quality or
the integrity of
the civil service

New public management (NPM) is measured indirectly as the mobility of high-level personnel between public and private sectors. This captures an important effect of NPM, namely, the emphasis on equal pay for identical jobs, whether in the public or the private sector, thereby encouraging mobility of officials between the two sectors. In contrast, the rewards and functions of senior officials in a traditional, career-based civil service are very different from those of their counterparts in the private sector, making it difficult for staff to move between the two sectors. The NPM variable is also not a significant determinant of the quality or the integrity of the civil service for the countries in the sample.

A trade-off exists
between the level of
wages and the number
of employees, yet . . .

There appears to be a strong relationship between the average *public sector wage* (relative to nominal per capita income) and the level of *public sector employment* (size of public sector relative to population), controlling for the level of development (purchasing power parity income per capita). The association with the average wage is negative, both for public sector employment and for the control variable, per capita income. Both results are highly statistically significant, and the negative signs are expected. These findings seem to provide compelling evidence for the existence of a negative relationship or trade-off between public sector employment and public sector wages: because of budget constraints, governments that increase the number of public sector workers are under pressure to lower salaries paid to them.

Nonetheless, impressive as the statistical results are, the evidence is quite weak because of limitations in the underlying data. In addition to large gaps in coverage, the data have two major defects. First, non-wage remuneration, such as pensions and automobiles, are excluded even though their value often exceeds that of the basic salary. Second, the definition of the public sector varies from country to country and sometimes even from year to year. Until governments make available better and more detailed information on remuneration paid to public servants, statistical findings must only be interpreted as suggestive, subject to confirmation or rejection in light of further evidence.

. . . the underlying data are weak

Prestige of a public sector career

Many governments face difficulties in recruiting and retaining well-educated civil servants, a problem often associated with low prestige of the public service.[6] Some governments find the task of recruitment more difficult than others. What accounts for this inter-country variation in the attractiveness of a career in the civil service? The survey questions dealt with the attractiveness of a public sector career to graduates of elite universities and to members of the educated middle class unable to attend elite schools.

The analysis suggests that a career in the public sector is more attractive the lower the per capita income of a country, presumably because low-income countries offer fewer opportunities for employment in their underdeveloped private sectors. For non-African countries, higher salaries increase the attraction of public service employment while reliance on income from extra-legal tips and bribes has the opposite effect. Prestige clearly increases with salary for the non-African sample, whereas in the African sample, there is no apparent relationship between the two variables. It is puzzling that legal remuneration has no impact on the attractiveness of public sector employment in the African countries in the sample. The analysis offers no explanation for this finding.

Even more surprising and disturbing is the finding that the level of bribes has no effect on the attractiveness of employment in the civil service in African countries in the sample. Other things being equal, high levels of extra-legal payments would be expected to impact negatively on the attractiveness of a career in the public sector, at least for university graduates with high ethical standards.

The existence of entrance examinations combined with university credentials enhances the prestige and attraction of a career in the public service. A higher proportion of university graduates among those who enter the civil service without writing an examination makes a civil service career *less* attractive to university graduates. This seems counter-intuitive at first glance, but on reflection, it is understandable that university graduates may prefer a work environment where the university educated are few in number, thereby making their credentials more valuable and visible.

New public management, indirectly measured as the mixing of professionals between private and public sector employment, is a significant negative determinant of the prestige of a public service career for recent university graduates, but weaker and less significant for African than for non-African countries (scatter plot 5).

A career in the public service is more attractive in low-income countries

For non-African countries, the attractiveness of a career in the public service suffers from bribes, yet . . .

. . . for African countries bribes are not a deterrent

Entrance examinations combined with university credentials enhance the prestige of a career in the public service

NPM has a negative impact on the prestige of a public sector career

Scatter plot 5.
Prestige and new public management

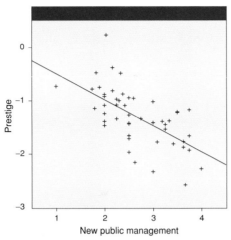

Source: UN/DESA.

Note: Plot of prestige against new public management
in 1970–1990 (51 countries), controlling for selected
variables.

Promotion to high-level political posts

A career-oriented,
merit-driven civil
service is attractive to
politicians as a source
of candidates for
placement in high-level
political posts

The quantitative analysis also looked at factors that influence the attractiveness *to politicians* of placing civil servants in high-level political posts. The results suggest that a traditional, career-oriented, merit-driven civil service is attractive to politicians as a source of candidates for placement in such posts. Surprisingly, there is no significant association at all between legal remuneration of top civil servants and their success in securing promotion to high-level political office.

In non-African
countries, bribes
received by senior
officials diminish the
probability that they
will be appointed to
political posts, . . .

. . . whereas the
opposite holds true for
African countries

The dichotomy between African and non-African countries with respect to the impact of bribes on selection is astounding. In the non-African sample, extra-legal income received by high-level public officials diminishes the probability that they will be appointed to political posts. In the 23 African countries, the effect of bribes is precisely the opposite: the attraction to politicians of placing civil servants in high-level political posts and corruption in the civil service go hand in hand.

However, the measure of income from tips and bribes is very crude. Some of the several "zero" observations might well be positive if the measures were finer, and the distribution of observations up and down the zero axis also makes it difficult to produce a significant slope for the relationship between bribes and promotion.

The proxy for NPM also has a negative effect on the probability that civil servants were promoted to high political office, but this is true only for the non-African countries in the sample, not for the 23 African countries, where the correlation is essentially zero.

Notes

1   For the complete background paper, see http://www.unpan.org/dpepa_worldpareport.asp

2   International Country Risk Guide. Researcher's Dataset (1984–present). PRS Group. Available from http://www.prsgroup.com/icrg/icrg.html.

3   Bates, Robert H. and others (2003). Political instability task force report: phase IV findings. McLean, VA: Science Applications International Corporation.

4   Rauch, James E. and Peter Evans (2000). Bureaucratic structure and bureaucratic performance in less developed countries. *Journal of Public Economics,* vol. 75, No. 1 (January), pp. 49–71. See also Peter Evans and James E. Rauch (1999). Bureaucracy and growth: a cross-national analysis of the effects of "Weberian" state structures on economic growth. *American Sociological Review,* vol. 64, no. 5 (October).

5   Court, Julius, Petra Kristen and Beatrice Weder (1999). Bureaucratic structure and performance: first Africa survey results (draft of 20 December). Available from http://www.unu.edu/hq/academic/Pg_area4/pdf/unu-research.pdf

6   Organisation for Economic Co-operation and Development (2002). Public service as an employer of choice. Paris: OECD. Available from http://www.oecd.org/document/10/0,2340,en_2649_201185_2095050_1_1_1_1,00.html

Bibliography

Boxes

1. Information and communication technologies

Bellamy, Christine and John A. Taylor (1998). *Governing in the Information Age.* Buckingham: Open University Press.

Organisation for Economic Co-operation and Development (2003). The e-Government Imperative. OECD e-Government Studies. Paris: OECD.

United Nations (2004). Global E-Government Readiness Report 2004: Towards Access for Opportunity. Department of Economic and Social Affairs. Available from http://unpan1.un.org/intradoc/groups/public/documents/un/unpan019207.pdf

_____ (2003). *World Public Sector Report: E-Government at the Crossroads.* Department of Economic and Social Affairs. Sales No. E.03.II.H.3.

2. UN/DESA analysis of government performance

See "Technical summary".

3. Benin

Kiragu, Kithinji and Rwekaza Mukandala (2004). Pay reform and policies report. Development Assistance Committee. Paris: Organisation for Economic Co-operation and Development.

Nelsen, Joan M., ed. (1990). *Economic crisis and policy choice.* Princeton, NJ: Princeton University Press.

4. China

Eberstadt, Nicholas (1998). China's new population problem. *The American Enterprise,* (July/Aug.). Available from http://www.taemag.com/docLib/20030717_chinasnew.pdf

Jackson, Richard and Neil Howe (2004). The graying of the Middle Kingdom: the demographics and economics of retirement policy in China. Center for Strategic and International Studies. Available from http://www.csis.org/gai/dc04/jackson-howe.pdf

Jincheng, Li (2003). China's human resources development and public sector reform facing economic globalization. 19th General Assembly and Conference of EROPA. (November). Available from http://unpan1.un.org/intradoc/groups/public/documents/EROPA/UNPAN014255.pdf

MingShan, Qi (2004). The study on Chinese civil servants' stimulation mechanism—taking Beijing city servants as the case. Selected papers by the Civil Service Commission of the Republic of Korea. Available from http://unpan1.un.org/intradoc/groups/public/documents/APCITY/UNPAN017082.pdf

United Nations (2003). *World Population Prospects: The 2002 Revision. Supplementary Tabulations.* (POP/DB/WPP/Rev.2002/1). CD-ROM.

Xiao, Li (2003). Human resources: key to economic development. *China.org.cn.* 17 April. Available from http://www1.china.org.cn/english/2003/Apr/62505.htm

5. Brazil

Bonturi, Marcos (2002). *The Brazilian Pension System: Recent Reforms and Challenges Ahead.* Economics Department Working Papers No. 340. Organisation for Economic Co-operation and Development. Available from http://appli1.oecd.org/olis/2002doc.nsf/linkto/eco-wkp(2002)26/$FILE/JT00130533.PDF

Ghilarducci, Teresa (1997). Do the old eat the young? Intergenerational equity and public pensions. Draft 1. Second International Research Conference on Social Security. Jerusalem, 25–28 January 1998. Available from http://www.issa.int/pdf/jeru98/theme3/3-6a.pdf

Government of Brazil (2002). Civil servants: continuity and change. Ministry of Planning. Available from http://www.planejamento.gov.br/arquivos_down/assec/serv_publ_continuidade_mudanca_ingles.pdf

_____ (2004). *Statistical Bulletin of Personnel,* vol. 104. Ministry of Planning. Available from http://www.servidor.gov.br/arq_editaveis/pdf/publicacoes/boletim/Bol104_dez2004.pdf

Knight, Peter T. (2004). E-gov.br—Operational lessons from Brazilian experience. Presentation at the World Bank. 12 April. Available from http://www.tedbr.com/apresentacoes/e-gov.br/e-gov.br-wb-bbl_12-04-04_files/frame.htm

Medici, André (2003). The political economy of pensions reforms: the case of civil servants in Brazil. Barbados: Inter-American Development Bank. Available from http://www.iadb.org/sds/doc/IFM-2003-Andr%C3%A9_Medici-E.ppt

Rabelo, Flavio M. (2004). The impact of ageing on the future of civil service. Presentation at the Ad Hoc Expert Group Meeting, "Unlocking the Human Potential for Public Sector Performance." Florence, 6–8 May. Available from http://unpan1.un.org/intradoc/groups/public/documents/un/unpan016603.pdf

Truglia, Vincent J. (2004). The Effects of Aging on Public Sector Pensions and Healthcare Systems: A Rating Agency Perspective. Prepared for the Senate Special Committee on Aging. Available from http://aging.senate.gov/_files/hr123vt.pdf

World Bank (2001). Brazil—Critical Issues in Social Security. A World Bank Country Study. Available from http://www-wds.worldbank.org/servlet/WDS_IBank_Servlet?pcont=details &eid=0000 94946_0107180400502

_____ (2002). Project Appraisal Document on a Proposed Loan in the Amount of US$5 Million to the Federative Republic of Brazil for Municipal Pension Reform Project. Report No. 24387 BR. Available from http://www-wds.worldbank.org/servlet/WDS_IBank_Servlet?pcont=details&eid=000094946_020 71104013783

6. Philippines

Adams, Jr., Richard H. (2003). *International Migration, Remittances, and the Brain Drain: A Study of 24 Labor Exporting Countries.* Policy Research Working Paper 3069. World Bank. Available from http://www-wds.worldbank.org/servlet/WDS_IBank_Servlet?pcont=details& eid=000094946_03062104301450

Alburo, Florian A. and Danilo O. Abella (2002). *Skilled Labor Migration from Developing Countries: Study on Philippines.* International Migration Papers 51. International Labour Organization. Available from http://www.ilo.org/public/english/ protection/migrant/download/imp/imp51e.pdf

Central Bank of the Philippines (2005). Press releases: 15 February 2005 and 15 March 2005. Available from http://www.bsp.gov.ph/news/news.htm

Ellerman, David (2003). *Policy Research on Migration and Development.* Policy Research Working Paper 3117. World Bank. Available from http://econ.worldbank.org/ files/29100_wps_3117.pdf

Hamilton, Kimberly (2003). Migration and development: blind faith and hard-to-find facts. Migration Information Source. Available from http://www.migration information.org/Feature/ display.cfm?id=174

Nyberg, Ninna (2004). *The Development Dimension of Migrant Remittances.* Migration Policy Research, Working Paper Series No. 1. International Organization for Migration. Available from http://www.iom.int/DOCUMENTS/ PUBLICATION/EN/mpr1.pdf

O'Neil, Kevin (2004). Labor export as government policy: the case of the Philippines. Migration Information Source. Available from http://www.migration information.org/Feature/ display.cfm?id=191

Ramamurthy, Bhargavi (2003). Migration and labour source countries: brain drain, remittances and the labour market. Institute for Future Studies, Sweden. Available from http://www.framtids studier.se/eng/globalMobReg/Bhargavipaper.pdf

7. South Africa

Bhorat, Haroon and others (2002). *Skilled Labour Migration from Developing Countries: Study on South and Southern Africa.* International Migration Papers 52. International Labour Organization. Available from http://www.ilo.org/ public/english/protection/migrant/download/imp/ imp52e.pdf

Cohen, Robin (1996). Brain drain migration. South African Commission on International Migration 1996–1997, Southern African Migration Project. Available from http://www.queensu.ca/samp/ transform/Cohen1.htm

Crush, Jonathan (2002). Nationalism, globalization and the South African brain drain. In *Journal of International Affairs,* vol. 56, No. 1, pp. 147–172. Available from http://jia.sipa.columbia.edu/journal.html

_____ (ed.) (2000). *Losing Our Minds: Skills Migration and the South African Brain Drain.* Migration Policy Series No. 18. Southern African Migration Project. Available from http://www.queensu.ca/samp/sampresources/samppublications/ policyseries/Acrobat18.pdf

Kaplan, David and others (2002). Brain drain: new data, new options. South African Network of Skills Abroad, National Research Foundation. Available from http://sansa.nrf.ac.za/documents/tradmon.pdf

Mattes, Robert and others (2000). *The Brain Gain: Skilled Migrants and Immigration Policy in Post-Apartheid South Africa.* Migration Policy Series No. 20. Southern African Migration Project. Available from http://www.queensu.ca/samp/sampresources/ samppublications/policyseries/Acrobat20.pdf

Myburgh, Andrew (2002). Globalization, labor mobility and the economics of emigration: the case of South Africa. Trade and International Policy Strategies—2002 Annual Forum. Available from http://www.queensu.ca/samp/migrationresources/braindrain/documents/myburgh.pdf

National Research Foundation (2003). Brain-drain and -gain in South Africa: who loses, who gains? Available from http://www.nrf.ac.za/news/braindrain.stm

Organisation for Economic Co-operation and Development (2004). The international mobility of health professionals: an evaluation and analysis based on the case of South Africa. Part III. In *Trends in International Migration: SOPEMI 2003 edition.* Available from http://213.253.134.29/oecd/pdfs/browseit/8104011E.PDF

8. Malawi

Bennell, Paul (2003). HIV/AIDS in Sub-Saharan Africa: the growing epidemic? Available from http://www.eldis.org/fulltext/BennellHIVAfrica.pdf

Government of Malawi (2000). The national strategic framework for HIV/AIDS 2000–2004. Available from http://hivaidsclearinghouse.unesco.org/ev_en.php?ID=2204_201&ID2=DO_TOPIC

_____ and United Nations Development Programme (2002). *The Impact of HIV/AIDS on Human Resources in the Malawi Public Sector.* Available from http://hivaids clearinghouse.unesco.org/ ev_en.php?ID=2214_201&ID2=DO_TOPIC

Joint United Nations Programme on HIV/AIDS (2004). *2004 Report on the Global AIDS Epidemic: 4th Global Report.* Geneva: UNAIDS. Available from http://www.unaids.org/bangkok2004/GAR2004_html/GAR2004_00_en.htm

Mwale, Biziwick (2002). NAC: How to cope with competing and numerous priorities? Where does TB/HIV fit in? Presentation at the Second Meeting of the Global Working Group on TB/HIV. Durban, South Africa, 14–16 June. Available from http://www.who.int/docstore/gtb/meetings/durban/June15/Afternoon/mwale.ppt

World Heath Organization (2002). Second meeting of the Global Working Group on TB/HIV. Durban, South Africa, 14–16 June. Available from http://www.who.int/docstore/gtb/publications/ tb_hiv/2003_311/wkg_gp_mtg2_tbhiv.pdf

9. United Kingdom

Accenture (2003). *Outsourcing in Government: Pathways to Value.* The Government Executive Series. Available from http://www.accenture.com/xdoc/en/industries/government/insights/ outsourcing_2003_report.pdf

European Commission (2004). UK public sector outsourcing set for dramatic rise, says new research. eGovernment News. Interoperable Delivery of European eGovernment Services to Public Administrations, Business and Citizens. Available from http://europa.eu.int/idabc/en/document/3667/5718

Government of the United Kingdom (2003). Treatment centres—a new service model. NHS Modernization Agency. Department of Health. Available from http://www.modern.nhs.uk/scripts/ default.asp?site_id=31&id=13854

Kable (2004). Public sector outsourcing 2000–2006. Available from http://www.kablenet.com/kd.nsf/ b7a6212a21220b0680256e85005a6581/$FILE/outsourcingTo2006 contents.pdf

_____ 2004). UK public sector outsourcing: the big picture 2007/2008. Available from http://www.kablenet.com/ kd.nsf/020781ea9db2becf80256f2a0051cf72/ $FILE/outsourcing2004contents.pdf

UNISON (2002). Diagnostic and treatment centres—preferred bidders. Available from http://www.unison.org.uk/bargaining/doc_view.asp?did=993

Xansa (2004). Xansa signs contract with the Department of Health to establish joint venture for the provision of finance and accounting services to the NHS. Press Release. 22 November. Available from http://www.xansa.com/multimedia repository/pdfs/167882.pdf

10. Mauritius

Bohnet, Iris and Susan C. Eaton (2003). Does performance pay perform? Conditions for success in the public sector. In John D. Donahue and Joseph S. Nye Jr., eds. *For the People: Can We Fix Public Service?* Harrisonburg, VA: Brookings Institution Press. Available from http://www.ksg.harvard.edu/visions/ deans_research_seminar/for_the_people_chpt_13.pdf

Cardona, Francisco (2002). Performance related pay in the public service. Second conference of the Institute of Public Administration and European Integration. Organisation for Economic Co-operation and Development/SIGMA. Available from http://www.psa.org.nz/library

Day, Jonathan D. and others (2002). Has pay for performance had its day? *The McKinsey Journal,* No. 4.

de Silva, Sriyan R. (1998). An introduction to performance and skill-based pay systems. Bureau for Employers' Activities, International Labour Organization. Available from http://www.ilo.org/public/english/dialogue/actemp/papers/1998/srspaysy.htm

Government of Mauritius (2003). *Review of Pay and Grading Structures and Conditions of Service in the Public Sector,* vol. 1. Pay Research Bureau, Prime Minister's Office. Available from http://ncb.intnet.mu /dha/prb/report03/

Grote, Dick (2000). What do we buy when we . . . Pay for performance? *Benefits and Compensation Solutions* (June). Available from http://www.cityofws.org/ training/performance/perf/pay.htm

Houston, David J. (2000). Public-service motivation: a multivariate test. *Journal of Public Administration Research and Theory,* vol. 10, issue 4, pp. 665–684. Lawrence.

Katz, Nancy R. (2000). *Incentives and Performance Management in the Public Sector.* Working Paper Series No. 2. JFK School of Government, Harvard University. Available from http://www.ksg.harvard.edu/visions/performance_management/ katz_incentives.htm

11. Canada

Government of Canada. Public Service Commission. Available from http://www.psc-cfp.gc.ca

_____ Implementation of the New Public Service Employment Act. Available from http://www.psc-cfp.gc.ca/psea-lefp/ index_e.htm

12. Cameroon

Government of Cameroon (2001). Deconcentration of the Management of State Personnel. SIGIPES Information Sheet. Yaoundé: Ministry of Public Service and Administrative Reform.

_____ (2003). *The Devolution of the Management of State Human Resources and SIGIPES.* Yaoundé: Ministry of Public Service and Administrative Reform.

Ndam, Gérard Pekassa (2004). The "new clothes" of administrative control of information-providing organizations in Cameroon since the 1990 reform. *International Review of Administrative Sciences,* vol. 70, issue 3.

Tazo, Olivier K. (2003). SIGIPES & aquarium: more transparent handling of personnel files in Cameroon. eTransparency Case Study No. 4. eGovernment for Development. Available from http://www.egov4dev.org/sigipes.htm

13. India

Banknet India (2000). Voluntary retirement & sabbatical scheme for public sector banks. Available from http://www.banknetindia.com/banking/vrs.htm

Dutta, Indrani (2003). CESC VRS: Early bird scheme evokes good response. *The Hindu: Business Line,* Nov. 12. Available from http://www.blonnet.com/2003/11/13/stories/2003111301560200.htm

Henkens, Kène and Hendrik P. van Dalen (2002). Early retirement systems and behavior in an international perspective. Available from http://www.seor.nl/ecri/pdf/henkensvandalenhandbook.pdf

Jain, Shweta and Gouri Shukla (2002). A not-so-golden handshake. *Business Standard: The Strategist,* Oct. 8. Available from http://www.banknetindia.com/issues/bsvrs.htm

Sridhar, V. (2001). Undermining banks' role. *Frontline,* vol. 18, No. 4, Feb. 17–Mar. 2, 2001. Available from http://www.flonnet.com/fl1804/18040490.htm

State Government of Orissa (2002). Orissa Public Enterprise Reform Programme. Department of Public Enterprises. Available from http://orissagov.nic.in/pe/programmes.htm

Supraja, Charumati (2002). The retirement rush. *The Hindu,* Oct. 24. Available from http://www.hindu.com/thehindu/mp/2002/10/24/stories/2002102400040200.htm

Thaur, B.S. (2002). VRS: where government failed. *The Tribune,* Dec. 26. Available from http://www.tribuneindia.com/2002/20021226/biz.htm#3

United Nations Development Programme (1999). *Public Sector Downsizing: Early Retirement Schemes and Voluntary Severance Pay.* Arab States Subregional Resource Facility. Beirut. Available from http://www.surf-as.org/Papers/downsize.pdf

14. Uruguay

Constance, Paul (2002). Just don't call it downsizing. *IDB America,* Magazine of the Inter-American Development Bank. Available from http://www.iadb.org/idbamerica/English/SRGOVE/srgove2.html

15. Germany

European Union (2004). 3rd Quality Conference for Public Administrations in the EU. Directors General of Public Administration of the EU. Available from http://www.3qconference.org/

16. Namibia

Jones, Merrick L. (2001). Sustainable organizational capacity building: is organizational learning key? *International Journal of Human Resource Management,* vol. 12, issue 1, Feb. 2001.

_____ and Peter Blunt (1999). "Twinning" as a method of sustainable institutional capacity building. *Public Administration and Development,* vol. 19, issue 1, Feb. 1999.

Litho in United Nations, New York
31833—October 2005—5M
ISBN 92-1-123155-8

United Nations publication
Sales No. E.05.II.H.5
ST/ESA/PAD/SER.E/63